PRIDE OF THE MARINES

Andrew Geer

Introduction by Lieutenant General R. McC. Pate, USMC
Foreword by Major General E. A. Pollock, USMC

First published by E P Button & Company in 1955.

This edition published in 2017.

TABLE OF CONTENTS

INTRODUCTION

I first heard of Reckless shortly after joining the 1st Marine Division in Korea in June of 1953. I was told she was a beautiful little mare with the head of a thoroughbred, but my first reaction was that this was probably an exaggeration, as I had seen many of the horses from past service in the Far East and knew them to be the Mongolian type of pony. I was also told of her heroic behavior in the battle of Vegas. Some of the tales I heard were difficult to believe.

I first saw this little lady, however, when the Division was in reserve for a brief period. After many, many months of close and bloody contact with the Chinese enemy, the Marines were given a respite from war. There was time to relax. A carnival was organized and a vast field was converted to an area where games of chance were operated. The profits from this venture were to go to Navy Relief.

It was then that I first saw Reckless. I was surprised at her beauty and intelligence, and believe it or not, her esprit de corps. Like any other Marine, she was enjoying a bottle of beer with her comrades. She was constantly the center of attraction and was fully aware of her importance. If she failed to receive the attention she felt her due, she would deliberately walk into a group of Marines and, in effect, enter the conversation. It was obvious the Marines loved her.

Within a few days of the carnival the 1st Marine Division went back into the line and once again Reckless performed with a courage and spirit that was difficult to understand or believe. Later, after the fighting had stopped, I was invited to attend a formal ceremony where Reckless was cited for bravery and I had the pleasure of promoting her to the rank of sergeant. Still later, there was another fundraising campaign in connection with the Iwo Jima Memorial. Many ideas were initiated to promote competition among units to see which could raise the most money. Suddenly Reckless was "kidnapped" and held for considerable ransom. The news swept the Division like wildfire. Needless to say, her ransom was quickly forthcoming and the fund over-subscribed.

In my career I have seen many animals that have been adopted by Marines, but never in all my experience have I seen one which won the hearts of so many as did this lovely little lady known as Reckless.

RANDOLPH McC. PATE, Lieutenant General, USMC
Assistant Commandant of the Marine Corps
Washington, D. C

FOREWORD

When I first heard about Reckless, it was shortly after she was purchased in October 1952. I thought it was an excellent idea. Sometimes Marines do weird things and adopt unusual pets. This time it was a horse, but when she was purchased the thought never occurred to Lt. Eric Pedersen that he was thereby establishing another great tradition for the Marine Corps. Nor did he realize the fame and publicity that this little horse would get. (She had once been a race horse destined for the track at Seoul.) Everywhere the Recoilless Rifle Platoon, 5th Marines, went, Reckless went along, even on maneuvers.

Pedersen paid $250 for the animal and the investment was returned in one battle. It would be difficult to say which side was more surprised, the Chinese or Marines, to see that horse charging up Outpost Vegas carrying ammunition. It was in this battle that she became a heroine and earned the love and respect of all Marines in the 5th and 7th Marines, and mine too. She carried more than 150 rounds of 75mm recoilless ammunition for the company from the dump to firing positions on Hill 120, and once served as a shield for four Marines working their way up the slope. Since it was after dark Reckless also earned the title of "Nightmare." She made most of her races after dark.

When I first saw Reckless she was behind the 5th Marines line in Panmunjom — Hill 229 — Bunker Hill Sector. This was sometime during the latter part of October or November 1952. She was not doing anything exceptional beyond receiving praise, food, and adoration from a group of Marines.

Naturally at this time I did not visualize the extent of her fame and fortune. I did realize, however, that any little morale factor would be a help and I considered the purchase of Reckless such a factor. This was at the time that we were being hit hard and regularly by the Chinese. Anything to maintain the already high morale was most welcome.

It was reported in the Division that Reckless, winner of the Paddy Derby at Vegas, challenged Native Dancer, victor in the Preakness at Pimlico, to a run. As a further indication of the morale value I understand that the men of the Special Weapons Company chipped in to buy Reckless for the entire unit.

Lt. Pedersen deserves full credit for the purchase of Reckless, the attending fame, and the good publicity for the Marine Corps. But more than that, when he obtained this horse, he was thinking only of his men, trying to save them from the back-breaking loads over extremely rugged and difficult terrain. I am sure also, that he was thinking of saving the lives of his weary ammunition carriers. This is all a part of good leadership. Reckless no doubt was imbued with this same spirit, because she became a true Marine.

EDWARD A, POLLOCK, Major General, USMC
Commanding General Marine Corps Recruit Depot
Parris Island, South Carolina

AUTHOR'S NOTE

From the day Reckless joined the Marine Corps, her story was bound to be written and I am happy the task fell to me. A great deal of luck was involved. With Korea well covered by writers, it is strange one of them did not seize upon her. Several times, when the fighting was slack, I attempted to steer visiting journalists her way, but never raised more than a flicker of interest. To nomadic newsmen, looking for a spot story before moving to another sector, Reckless was not news.

To the casual observer, she was just another horse. To me, who had been born into a horse-loving family and who had owned his first at the age of nine, she displayed attributes and intelligence never before seen in an animal. From the day I joined the 5th Marines to command the Second Battalion, I knew I would one day write about this little red horse. It would take time, however, for I had made it a policy not to write while fighting, though I will admit to taking a few notes along the way. Some war stories become dated, but in the case of Reckless there was no such worry. Her story is as timeless as that of Black Beauty.

In Part II of the story is the account of my having lunch with Ben Hibbs of the *Saturday Evening Post* and his Instant recognition of her story value. The *Post* carried the article in April, 1954, and in May Elliott Macrae, president of Button, cabled from Europe asking that I do a book, on the same subject. Subsequently, three other publishers sought similar books. Reckless was becoming known.

Three tours of duty in the Korean war theater had given me a deep compassion for the people of Chosen, which will become obvious to the reader. In the months following the truce, while with my regiment on the Kimpo Peninsula, there was time to search out the story. Except for stray bits of information which could be gotten by mail, most of the research had been done when Elliott Macrae asked for a book.

The life of the Korean people under Japanese domination is as true as long hours of digging would uncover. It was slow going over the language barrier and the bridge built by unskilled interpreters was ofttimes weak. Certain shadings and alterations to the story have been made at the request of the youth I call Kim Huk Moon.

In the writing of a book of this kind there are many deserving of thanks. These are due Ernest Gibson and Stan Coppel for making Reckless' sea trip from Yokohama to San Francisco possible without its being a financial burden. Gordon Jones, Pacific Transport Lines representative in Yokohama, saw to the details of hay, grain and a salt lick, while Captain Kenneth Shannon, master of the vessel, afforded his passenger every kindness. These are the men who provided the book with a happy ending.

Particular thanks are due Lew Walt for the completeness with which he answered many questions on the Battle for Vegas and the cooperation given by Brute Krulak and Pete Stephan. A debt is owed Al Gentleman and Ed Wheeler for reporting several unusual stories about Reckless, and to Prank Garretson and Harry Edwards at Headquarters Marine Corps, who were called on many times and never failed.

There will always be a warm spot at my hearth for Jim Michener, who kept me informed as to Reckless' welfare after my departure from Korea; and for Walter Pickerell who journeyed to the Seoul race track and took snapshots and reported on current conditions at the new track; and Edna Clem, of the Historical Section at Headquarters Marine Corps, who was always prompt in checking the records on personnel queries.

And now we come to the Marines who were closest to Reckless: Eric Pedersen, Bill Riley, Joe Latham and Elmer Lively. Without them the story could not have been written and I hope they are pleased with the result.

ANDREW GEER
San Francisco
Feb. 22, 1955

PART ONE

CHAPTER I

THE STORY OF RECKLESS begins with a young Korean boy, Kim Huk Moon, who loved horses. Ever since Kim was eight years old he had wanted to own a horse. Night after night he put himself to sleep dreaming of the horse he would one day own. Kim's dream did not spring on him from the darkness like a tiger from a thicket. It came to him on the day of his grandfather's funeral. Word reached the family in the middle of the night that Grandfather Kim had died, and early the next morning they started out to make the journey across the city of Seoul. Father Kim, silent and sad-faced, led the way, followed by Mother Kim and Nam Soon, and last were Chung Soon and Kim.

At the corner of the five streets, tall, stern Schoolmaster Yu was waiting and he fell in stride with Father Kim. With their backs to the sun and the Han River, they walked through the village. A shrill-voiced old woman, sitting with her back to a cracked mud and wattle hut, cried out at them. Father Kim and Yu bowed and walked on. Then they were free of the buildings and the road lost itself among the hills. It was not long before the hills fell away into the flat lands of the rice paddies and mulberry orchards, and everywhere there was motion with serpentine lines of people and horse carts, workers in the paddy fields and orchards and the morning wind in the young rice.

By the roadside sat a Buddhist monk, bathing his feet in a paddy stream. When he saw Father Kim approaching he dried his feet and rose to greet him. His face was leathery, seamed and ugly, but his eyes were calm and kind and he let his cool hand rest on Kim's head. Three abreast, the men led the way and in a half mile came to the streetcar line.

Kim sat beside the tram window while Chung Soon pointed out the sights. There was the Kyongsong Athletic Field with Japanese boys in white uniforms at play, and closer to the tracks there was a Buddhist temple. The holy man leaned far out the window and stared while Chung Soon alerted Kim to watch for the riding academy so that he might see the cavalry squadron drilling with sabers flashing in the sun.

Kim's father spat, as he always did when he saw Japanese troops.

The city grew heavy with buildings and thick with people. There was a halt, a wait, and then an imperious Japanese policeman with white sleeves waved them on. The tramcar turned north and Chung Soon told Kim, "Now we come to Chong-Ro. If you are quick you can see the Big Bell at the corner."

Shortly after, the car passed through West Gate and came to the end of the line where friends were waiting. The party walked toward the prison. The guards shouted at them, but after a time the body of Grandfather Kim was released and the procession moved back through the West Gate, past the police station on the corner and into the churchyard. Ever after that, death to Kim meant the burning of incense and the Buddhist priest chanting the Sutras and the fluttering of the prayer wheel in the wind.

Schoolmaster Yu and the holy man stayed behind at the temple when Father Kim led his family onto the city streets to catch a streetcar back to the village. The day was now hot and the streets crowded. In the confusion they boarded the wrong tram, but it went unnoticed until it failed to turn off Chong-Ro. It took a long time to work his way through the crowd to speak to the conductor while the car sped them farther and farther out of their way. Father Kim began shouting and shoving his way through the pack. In the midst of all this, sparks flew from the metal box near the motorman and the car screeched to a halt.

The motorman looked into the box and shrugged and the conductor seemed to hold Father Kim responsible for the power failure and ordered him off, but Kim's father argued that he should be repaid the fares. A Japanese official arrived and was angry with everyone. When Father Kim was pointed out as the troublemaker, the Japanese beat him over the shoulders with a cane. All Koreans were ordered to leave the area.

Because it was so hot, they sought the shade of the nearby grandstand of the Seoul race track. For the first time in his life Kim saw a race horse. He forgot the heat and his thirst as he stared at the horses galloping, their trim feet kicking up small puffballs of dust. He began to tremble and Chung Soon, seeing his agitation, spoke to Mother Kim. Fearing the boy had a fever, she wiped his face with a damp cloth and gave him a drink of water purchased from a vender.

One rider brought his horse close to the outer rail and called for water. The horse was a red sorrel with white stockings and a broad blaze down its nose. Hypnotized, Kim watched the animal.

Kim had to dogtrot to follow the resolute pace set by his angry father. As he trotted along he saw and heard a train moving north from the Yongdongpo Bridge. The train whistled in a petulant wail and a banner of smoke rose like a black ribbon in the still afternoon air. Always before such a sight had thrilled Kim, but today he scarcely saw it as his mind's eye was filled with the image of the horse.

At last they reached the shabby old mud and wattle hut. It was twin to a hundred others that lay side to side or back to back along the narrow, crooked streets that were red soil thrown over rocks. As the surface eroded, the rocks protruded like ugly moles and wracked the wheels of the night soil cart.

The Kim house formed an L. The roof was of rice straw, dark with mildew, and the walls were baked mud. Inside the house, beyond the flimsy, sagging door, was a platform of raised flooring which covered two-thirds of one wing. The baked mud stove with its elbow-jointed chimney was surprisingly efficient. Adjoining it was the sleeping kong, also of baked mud, with tunnels underneath in which fires could be built to warm the sleeping surface in winter. The shorter end of the L was without flooring or platform and was used for storage of wood and charcoal and the hanging of meat or fowl or fish, when the Kims were fortunate enough to come by such food. In each arm of the L there was one window opening, without frame or glass. In the winters these openings were covered over with rice straw matting.

Mother Kim hurried to the task of cheering her husband by serving him a fine meal. Because it was quick and soothing, she made soup from powdered soya beans. Then she would surprise everyone by serving Kimchee and, as an added fillip, she cooked rice to pack the unfilled corners of their stomachs. With a recklessness she had not shown before, she brewed tea from the hoarded pinches of China leaves. It was against the law to possess Chinese tea, but it was much tastier than the bitter, low-grade stuff forced on them by the Japanese. A Korean family was considered fortunate indeed to come by some. Mother Kim had a brother who worked on the docks at Inchon and had stolen several tins while unloading a Russian ship and he had given one to his sister. This occurred a year before Kim was born and now the metal container was about empty.

Mother Kim guardedly watched her husband as he squatted in the shade smoking his bamboo-stemmed pipe, coughing now and again with a sepulchral sound. He had not spoken since the train official beat him with the cane.

She knew there were welts across his shoulders, but these did not worry her; it was her concern to salve the hurt to his pride. The sipping of contraband Chinese tea would be an act of independence which would ease his hurt — not that a man could ever wholly forget such a thing.

"How long must we wait? How long can we wait?" he asked. She glanced fearfully toward the door as though she expected a Japanese policeman to be standing there listening.

"At each meeting they tell us to wait, that the League of Nations will do for us what we will not do for ourselves. Hah!" His voice grew angry, "While we wait, my father dies in prison. His crime was preaching freedom for the people of this land of Morning Calm. While we wait, our children go without schooling and are scrawny from empty stomachs."

Father Kim sucked on a dying pipe because he had only enough tobacco for an after-dinner smoke. "You and I work the fields the daylight hours and for our labors we receive less than enough to buy the rice to feed us and cotton cloth to cover our bodies. Today's tram ride cost us one yen twenty sen. I must work three days from dawn to dark for that amount, and with rice seventy sen a kilo, we have but enough for life. How long can we wait?" he repeated hopelessly. Further protest was smothered in a fit of coughing.

Shortly after they went to bed a wind went whistling through the streets, blowing clouds of dust before it and drawing in its wake a soft, gray rain. Kim heard the rain on the roof and turned its patter into the beat of a horse's hoofs. That night he had his first of ten thousand dreams about a horse that he would someday own. It was just such a horse as he had seen over the rail at the track. The dream was so vivid that he began to tremble in his sleep and Chung Soon held him tightly in her arms.

At the first hint of light in the sky to the east, Mother Kim was feeding twigs and small wood into the stove so that just enough fire was made to prepare the morning rice and heat water to drink.

When the sisters stepped outside with Kim, they saw their father already standing in the small triangle of land embraced by the two arms of the L. Wearing only a fundoshi, the muscles and bones of his thin body were rigidly defined through his taut, parchment-like skin. His spindly, muscle-knotted legs were braced against the hacking and spewing he must do to relieve his congested lungs. Before he was through he was sweating and exhausted.

Once he got his breath, he recited the Four Truths: "Birth is pain, old age is pain, sickness is pain and death is pain."

The morning meal consisted of a bowl of rice and many cups of hot water. As the rim of sun came over the hill the mother and father hurried to the fields. Chung Soon was left in charge. While Kim did small chores in the yard the two sisters aired the sleeping pads and cleaned the house and rinsed the rice bowls.

Kim wandered onto the street and his eyes turned in the direction of the race track as though drawn by a magnet. He began to run. From time to time he fell and his knees became scraped and bleeding. There were many people and carts on the road, but he pressed through and around them. At one time, far behind, he heard Chung Soon calling, but this he ignored and pressed on to his goal.

The morning sun was hot and he began to pant. He was nearly exhausted when the high wooden shell of the grandstand came into view. Completely done in, he reached the shadows of the vast structure and crawled into a shallow ditch by the outer rail and, sitting in the cool grass, watched the horses. His lips were stiff and his tongue thick from want of water, but he clung to his post. Many horses came onto the track and finally Kim was rewarded when he saw his dream horse circling toward him.

He was oblivious to a group of well-dressed Japanese men who came to the rail. The flame-colored horse with the white stockings and white ribbon down its face came to the outer rail while the rider talked with the man. If there was a single detail of the animal he had missed the previous day, it was burnt into his memory now.

The horse turned away and, circling into position in front of the group, spun off down the track at a run. To Kim it was the fastest movement he had ever seen, even faster than the Yongdongpo train. He held his breath for fear the horse might fall as he himself had fallen on the road. From the ditch all Kim could see was the rider's red cap bobbing along the rail at a fierce speed until the horse came into view at the upper end of the straight stretch. The horse passed by and slowed and came back to the rail while the men clustered around the one who held a shining metal disc in his hand. There was shouting and laughter at what they saw and the rider laughed with them. Sweating freely and with a rim of white lather under the leather reins, the horse was eager for more. She snorted and let out a deep sigh and Kim thought of his father when he went to the sleeping pad at night.

When the rider took the horse away toward the buildings on the far side of the track, the men called to a water vender and all drank thirstily. Kim watched and momentarily forgot about the horse and thought of the long walk home. He was badly frightened when he realized one of the Japanese was speaking to him. The man, taller than the others, was in uniform and his high, leather boots shone in the sun. Kim scrambled to his feet and stood stiffly at attention with his eyes to the ground as his father had taught him. Though Kim listened carefully, it was difficult to understand the man.

"Are you lost?"

Slowly Kim formed his reply, "No, Honored One, I live over there." He pointed.

"What are you doing in a ditch beside the track?"

"Watching, Honorable One."

"Watching what?"

"The horses." Kim lifted his eyes for a fleeting moment. "Watching the flame horse with the white legs, Honored One."

"Why that horse?" The voice was not so curt.

"It is the horse I sleep with." Kim had meant to say "dream of." The men laughed and he ducked his head lower in embarrassment.

"Why do you sleep with my horse?" The voice was nearly gentle now.

"It is the number one, Honorable One."

The Japanese was pleased and his gloved hand patted the top of Kim's head.

"You have a good eye for horses, little one." He called the water vender and ordered the man to serve the boy. Kim drank thirstily. When he was finally through, he took a deep, gasping breath and looked up at the man. He smiled briefly. The gloved hand came from a pocket and between the thumb and forefinger was a yen note. Kim looked into the face of his new friend before he could believe the money was to be his. He took it and bowed stiffly. When he straightened, the man and his group had turned away and were walking toward a long, black automobile waiting near the gate, Kim watched them until they had entered the machine and it moved out of sight.

Refreshed by the water and stunned by his good fortune, Kim turned his attention to the track again. There were few animals in sight now and his Flame was nowhere to be seen. He sat in the ditch and waited patiently, but as the sun grew warmer, fewer horses remained on the track. He wanted to go to the stables where the horses had disappeared, but was afraid. After a time, when he was certain no more horses would appear, he tucked the yen note in the toe of his rubber slipper and began the long walk home. Every now and again he would stop and look into his slipper to see that the yen note was safe.

In an open field he saw an ox walking a circle as it drew water from a well. He crossed to it and gaining permission from the boy tending the ox, knelt by the sluiceway and washed his face and the blood from his knees. As he reached the rim of the road again he heard the Yongdongpo train whistle and it was not long before he saw familiar faces. The old woman called to him in an angry voice.

"Are you not Kim Huk Moon?"

Kim stopped. With his big toe rubbing against the yen note he bowed to the old woman. "I am Kim Huk Moon."

"Your sisters have been looking for you. You ran away, you should be whipped. You are a bad one!"

Kim turned away, embarrassed with so many people staring at him as the old woman's shrill voice followed him down the crowded street. Then Chung Soon, red-faced from running, was beside him. She gave him a thoughtful look and taking his hand, they walked together along the street. They found Nam Soon waiting for them and she began to scold, but Chung Soon silenced her.

With reluctance and considerable care, Kim stepped out of his slippers at the door and wondered how he could claim the yen note without being seen. Chung Soon gave him a bowl of cold rice and while eating he sat where he could watch his slippers. When he was through, she unrolled a sleeping pad for him on the kong.

He fought to stay awake in the cool dimness of the room and forced his ears to follow the voices of his sisters. When he heard them playing hopscotch in the street he slipped from the sleeping pad and retrieved the money from his slipper. He went to sleep with it clutched tightly in his hand.

He was still tired when Chung Soon awakened him, but knew he must be up before his mother and father returned from the fields. While Chung Soon built up a small fire and began to heat water, Kim rolled the pad and put it against the wall. With the yen note still clutched in his hand, he went into the yard to look for a place to hide his fortune. He could see no place to his liking and the bill began to burn in his sweating palm. He went back inside. Nam Soon had gone to the riverbank to fish for stray bits of firewood and Chung Soon was busy with her chores. She squatted on her hunkers blowing life into the fire and smiled at him over her shoulder.

"Do you feel better, Little One?" she asked.

"I am still tired."

Chung Soon took a deep breath and poured it onto the smoldering fire. It came to life flaming. She said, "You play too hard; you run too much and fall down too often. That is why you are tired and your knees are raw."

Kim knew she was telling him no mention would be made of his absence. He held out his hand and opened it. She took the damp paper, straightened it and her eyes widened as she worked the creases from it carefully.

"I will put it in a safe place for you."

Kim followed as she hurried into the storeroom wing of the L. From a shelf she took a glass jar the Han River had brought them some days before. Removing the top, she dropped the money into it and then replaced the cover tightly. Together they placed the glass in a hole underneath the mud sill and covered it over.

When their parents entered the house they carried fagot bundles scavenged along the way and were slow-moving and weak from fatigue. As they were washing in the yard Nam Soon arrived with a timber she had found near the river's edge. It weighed nearly as much as she did and to get it home she almost had to crawl with it. It was a stroke of fortune that could not often happen with thousands of people searching the turgid water from its source to where it married up with the Yellow Sea. Such a piece of fuel would cook the rice, boil the water and heat the sleeping kong for a week during the winter.

Nam Soon had gone into the water up to her armpits to reach the timber and Father Kim cautioned her about going so far into the river.

The meal of rice and hot water was soon over. Because of their hard work in the fields, the mother and father shared a small portion of pickled fish from the stone crock in the storeroom. Father Kim also had a cup of Japanese tea to salve his tired muscles and ease his cough, which usually started up with the cool, moist air rising from the river. While Mother Kim and the two girls cleaned away after the meal and rolled out the sleeping pads, Father Kim went to the street side of the house and lighted his bamboo-stemmed pipe. Kim joined him with a kickball of cloth tightly bound around a cork stuck with four chicken tail feathers. He was clever with the ball and by striking it with his toe, heel or palm could keep the feathered thing in the air for long periods.

The agility of his son pleased but saddened Father Kim and he groaned as he faced up to the hopelessness of life. How could a man whose life savings were less than fifteen yen, send a son to school which cost fifty sen a month? His body would not stand longer hours in the fields and he thought of investing his small savings in rubber shoes and other wearing apparel and opening a little shop; the girls were old enough to tend it during the day. This idea was discarded when he looked along the street and realized that almost every neighbor had some sort of wares counter.

Father Kim knocked the ash from his pipe and rose to go to bed. Unless a man owned land, at least six tun, there was no future. He had told himself this every day since he was a young man about to marry, yet after fourteen years of hard work and thrift, he had but enough for rice and would never own land.

Two hours after the sun settled into the Yellow Sea, the hard-working Korean villagers were abed. The district was an assignment coveted by the Japanese police for there was no trouble and night patrols could go slack. In the station building adjoining the railway house the police could play cards or sleep the night through with ease of mind, for they knew their charges lacked the energy or spirit to foment trouble.

Tired as he was, Kim thought of the horse. Once again he lived through every moment of the day. When he finally slept it was to have a vivid dream of the red sorrel.

CHAPTER II

IN THE MORNING Kim was seized with an irresistible desire to return to the track and his eyes kept seeking the direction toward the high wooden stands. He tried to get excited over a game of kickball with a playmate from across the street, but his attention was so divided that he was beaten many times. He left the game and entered the house to find his sisters in the triangle of beaten earth washing the field clothes worn by their parents. Chung Soon's eyes lifted to meet his as she slap-slapped a wet garment on a rock. Kim turned away, passed through the house and onto the street. Without pause, he struck off for the track.

Chung Soon knew he was leaving and her heart was clutched with fear. Where was he going? What did he do? How had he come by the yen note?

"I must know where he goes, what he does."

Nam Soon answered shortly, "And I will be left with all the work."

"I will hurry. I will go into the hills searching for wood for you when I come back."

With Nam Soon's grumbling in her ears, Chung Soon hurried out and began to run toward the shrill-voiced woman's house near the intersection. She slackened her pace to a fast walk when she saw a policeman and lowered her eyes and walked stiffly by the man. Then she began to run again. She was at the five-street intersection before she saw Kim and slackened her pace to allow a discreet distance to remain between them.

Kim walked with assurance. Though the day was hot, it did not worry him and it was not long before he saw the grandstand looming in the distance, and then he was in its shade and at the track rail. There were many horses circling the oval, but a glance told him his horse was not out yet. He climbed to the top of the wooden rail and with his toes curled about the vertical pole he was secure and happy with the better view.

Chung Soon arrived at the track a few minutes after Kim and, clinging to the shadow of the structure, she gained a view of the track. She saw Kim perched on the railing, hunched over in a comfortable position with elbows on his knees and his chin cupped in his hands. She remembered how strangely affected he had been on the first day; she had thought it was fever, but it had been only the sight of the horses. He had been hypnotized by them.

Chung Soon turned to make her way home. All her questions had been answered save one. How had he come by the yen note? It could not have been in dishonest manner or he would not have returned. She sighed over her problem and hurried along the dusty road.

Kim waited patiently and he began to sec things that he had missed before. Some of the horses wore cloth wraps around their legs, others ran free of bandages. There were riders who appeared to float on the backs of their mounts like feathers while others jolted along like rocks. Once in a while the scene would become exciting as two riders challenged one another and let their mounts run full out for a short space.

Then his horse came onto the track! Instantly all the others were lost to view as he saw it come through the gate on the far side, and he gripped the pole tightly with his toes to keep from falling. The filly minced along the outside rail with her white stockings twinkling in the sunlight. Kim drank in every movement, every gesture and was happy when he saw the rider floating along with the horse, not seeming to touch it but as much a part of it as the neck or head.

Following the outside rail, the horse came within a few feet of him and he could smell the sweet grass fragrance and hear the rider soft-talking to it.

The Japanese rider saw the ragged little Korean on the fence and remembered him. When he nodded and spoke politely Kim nearly fell from his perch.

The horse circled the track at a slow pace and then was let out in a gallop. Twice around at this easy pace and then the rider took her to the middle of the track where he pulled his cap down and, crouching lower, let the eager animal out to a fast gallop. Once around at this speed and they left the track through the rear gateway. Kim was bereft at this sudden loss and looked longingly across the track. The temptation was too much.

His pace slowed as he crossed the track and his heart pounded the closer he approached, but his curiosity drove him on. He came to the rear gate and followed a road through the line of stalls until he saw his horse being rubbed vigorously. When the grooms were finished the flame-red coat shone like the sun in the early morning. A gnarled old man stood nearby with the rider, watching. The two carefully inspected the horse. A youth of twelve or thirteen came from the stable and, taking the lead rope in hand, began to walk the horse in a circle. His manner was bored, nonchalant and

Kim was instantly filled with a venomous hatred. He twisted and squirmed as he fought the urge to rush out and tear the rope from his hands.

All along the area between the mud-walled stables other horses were being saddled, rubbed or walked. A fiery stallion was brought from a stall. It reared high in the air lifting the man on the lead strap from the ground. Kim wished the rider would not get on this one. While one groom tried to quiet the wild horse, a second cupped his hands and the rider stepped into them and lifted himself easily, fearlessly onto the horse. Once he was in the saddle the stallion quieted somewhat and Kim breathed again. As the rider turned toward the track he noticed Kim, who braced himself stiffly and bowed formally.

He turned his attention to the flame-colored horse as the old man ran his hand under the blanket, feeling the neck, the shoulder and barrel. The filly nuzzled against him and Kim was happy that the horse had not shown such affection for the lead boy. The old man spoke in Japanese, which Kim could barely understand, and the boy led the horse into the stall.

Kim returned to the grandstand and paused in the shade; home seemed a long way off at the moment he noticed a small hole leading into the dark, cavernous section under the seats. With difficulty he squeezed through and when his eyes became accustomed to the darkness, he saw that the ground was littered with a confusion of things thrown down by the people who sat overhead. He began to paw about in this scavenger's delight. There were papers, bottles, age-hardened orange peels, apple cores and, find of finds, many saw ends of wood! Obviously, it was virgin territory.

The sight of this treasure did not throw Kim into a panic. He had been with his sisters on too many foraging expeditions not to know how to proceed. Selecting an area near the small hole where the light was better, he began to sort through the refuse methodically. The bottles, apple cores and orange peels were tossed into a discard pile. The papers were flattened and put one on the other and the pieces of wood went next to the paper. He came upon an eight-foot length of stout cord and his breath sucked in gustily at the sight of it.

He had worked his way through a forty-foot square when his fingers touched a metal disc. He rushed with it to the light. It was a fifty sen piece! He slipped it into his rubber slipper, panting a little from his good fortune. He looked into the deep cavern, each day he would sort through a section and carry paper and wood home, but any money he found would go into the jar and one day he would have enough to buy a horse.

Wrapping the wood in the paper, he formed a large bundle and secured it with the cord which was long enough to make knapsack loops for his shoulders. He was dismayed to find the bundle too large to shove through the hole. Patiently, he untied the cord and shoved the lot, piecemeal, through the opening and squeezed outside after it. Once again he tied the bundle and found he would have to walk nearly bent double to support it. Grimly he started out.

The sun was hot and soon he was sweating until it ran into his eyes, partially blinding him. Every time he stumbled the bundle was thrown from right or left and he would have to lunge in the direction of the load to regain the point of balance. His forward progress was punctuated by these tipsy maneuvers and his sidewise progress was nearly that of his movement forward. When he had gone as far as his legs would carry him, he staggered to a halt. The load overcoming him, he was pulled backwards and lay in the dusty road propped against the bundle. After a time he had the strength to slip his pinched shoulders from the cord and was embarrassed to see a knot of people gathering about him.

An elder asked, "Are you hurt, Small One?"

Kim scrambled to his feet and bowed, "The load is heavy. I am resting."

The old man nodded. "Do not lift your guts out. There is enough pain in life without that." He bowed and went on, followed by the curious. One avaricious-looking man remained nearby while Kim sat on the wood watching the fellow covertly. There were deep purple tattoo marks on his arms, neck and chin.

The man spoke, "May I help you with your heavy load?"

The words were Korean, but the voice was not: neither was it Japanese. Kim pretended to be entranced by the Yongdongpo train that was waving a black plume of smoke in the air on its way south toward the Han River, He well knew what such an offer meant: half the load at the end! He slid off the bundle until his buttocks rested on the road and began to fit his aching shoulders into the cord loops. As he strained back in an arch, the coin rolled from his rubber slipper and lay in the dust. Kim gasped and his hand darted out to grasp the coin and a handful of dust with it.

The man moved closer. His tongue ran over his blue lips. "That is much money for a young one to have. Where did you steal it? And the wood?" He leaned over until his face was but a foot from Kim's. "Give me the coin before I break your arm."

"Go away!" Kim shrieked. Startled, the man jumped back. Kim squirmed from his bindings, sprang to his feet and began to run on terror-driven legs. He cried out when he saw a number of people moving toward him along the road. His terror evaporated when Chung Soon broke from the crowd and came flying toward him with several neighbor men at her winged heels. Kim was surprised when Chung Soon and the men rushed right on by him and for the first time he realized his pursuer was not breathing down his neck. The tattooed man had picked up the bundle, but when he saw the wrathful vanguard descending, he dropped the wood and took off across the bordering rice paddy. No one followed.

Kim was so weak and shaky he had to sit down. Chung Soon placed the wood beside him and squatted so she could look into his face.

"Are you hurt, Little One?"

Kim shook his head, but did not look at her or try to speak. He continued to stare across the fields toward the Han River and the railway tracks. In the distance he could see the tattooed man still running toward the Yongdongpo Bridge. Chung Soon took a cloth from her belt and wiped his face and neck.

"Why do you go to the place where the horses run?"

Kim looked into her eyes and once more turned his gaze toward the river. Without replying he got to his feet and began to trudge down the road toward the village while Chung Soon took up the bundle and followed after.

The shrill-voiced old woman was waiting for them and her keen eyes ferreted Kim from the throng as he came around the bend of road. She could be heard above the noise of all else. Kim burned with embarrassment but Chung Soon at his shoulder, muttered, "Pay the Noisy One no heed."

Being ignored angered the woman more and her threats became active. "I know you, Kim Huk Moon, you are a lazy runaway. I will tell your father the trouble you cause your sister Chung Soon."

Kim was shaken by this for fear he would be prevented from returning to the track. The thought of not seeing his flame-colored horse again wrenched his heart until he let out a cry. Chung Soon put her free arm around him and hurried him along the street. There was only one more barrier to pass: at the intersection there was the Japanese policeman who ofttimes stopped people and inspected bundles. What could she tell the officer, where had they gotten the paper, wood and stout cord? They saw the policeman, standing with arms folded, in the center of the road and the flowing tide of people broke around him like water around a rock. The two slipped by in the current and once they were at a safe distance, wings touched their heels and they ran the remainder of the way home.

They arrived in the triangle of yard, breathless, Nam Soon was inclined to scold, but subsided at the sight of the wood and paper. As she began to build the small fire against the arrival of their parents. Chung Soon and Kim unwrapped the bundle in the storage room. The wood was stacked and the papers carefully folded to be looked at by Father Kim.

Chung Soon then considered Kim soberly. "What will we tell our father? He will ask about the paper, he will want to know."

Kim worried over the questions, but found no answer. He shook his head. Chung Soon said, "It fell from the train and rolled into the ditch?"

Kim nodded and held out the coin. Chung Soon's hand darted out and took it. She examined it closely and bit into it. She looked over her shoulder to sec where Nam Soon was before she handed it back.

"Put it with the other," she whispered.

Mother and Father Kim arrived from the fields. As usual, they were exhausted to the point of collapse. Their hand bath from the earthenware bowls in the yard refreshed them somewhat. As Father Kim got into dry clothing he saw the wood and papers and was pleased with such a windfall and patted Chung Soon on the shoulder.

While the evening meal was being prepared, he sat in the cooling breeze coming off the river and studied the papers carefully. His work-roughened forefinger moved slowly down the column of figures. When a spasm of coughing seized him, the finger would joggle up and down, losing his place, but this failed to bother him for he knew only a few of the characters. His reading consisted in searching the long columns for the few he knew.

He called Kim to him. "All men should know how to read and write."

Kim bowed. "Yes, Honored Father."

"Would you be awake and seize on each figure as you would a piece of fish if I make arrangements with the Honorable Yu Jik Soo?

Kim lowered his eyes to hide his panic. If he went to reading and writing, he could not go to the track. He asked shyly, "Why don't you teach me?"

His father coughed. "I know but a few characters, not enough to be of use." Father Kim lowered his voice, "I am the first in my family to be without this knowledge. It is the same with all since the Japanese came to our Land of Chosen. I will go to see Yu Jik Soo tonight."

Kim was in such a panic it was an effort to swallow his rice. After the sparse meal his father filled the long-stemmed pipe and left while Kim squatted against the wall of the hunt and waited.

Father Kim found Schoolmaster Yu seated on a rice straw mat gazing across the Han. The old scholar was an honored elder for risking imprisonment by conducting a Korean school. Father Kim spoke of being unable to read or write and his desire to have his son learn the characters.

Yu nodded in agreement. He removed the pipe stem from his thin, blue lips and his free hand stroked wisps of hair that hung from his chin like white silk threads.

"And so it is all over this sad Land of Chosen. We who love freedom and yearn for knowledge are stifled by cruel masters. We who printed our language in movable type before any other people and who had a phonetic alphabet five hundred years ago, will be a nation of illiterates in another twenty-five years." Yu's low, sonorous voice shook with emotion. "Your generation is nearly wordless, that of your son will be. Unless you are willing to send your son to a Japanese school to learn to worship a living man as a God, to bow his neck to the yoke. Through their schools they hope to bleed from our children the desire of freedom. "Then our Nippon masters will have reached their goal — those educated to their beliefs or human illiterates to grow rice and dig metals from the hills."

The old man filled and lighted his pipe. "My hours are filled with teaching the sons of a hundred fathers like yourself. This morning I could have taken no one — tonight, I can. The son of Wang Jin Won died of the coughing sickness today. Kim Huk Moon can take his place. He will have two hours a day, the hours between three and five in the afternoon. He will come alone, by the river pathway and he is to be warned of the risk I take."

Father Yu sucked in a deep breath of pleasure. The coolness of the night and dampness from the river set him to coughing. The spasm was as severe as he had ever experienced and Old Yu watched with concern. He was shaken with a deep compassion for this man and knew Kim could ill afford payment, no matter how little it might be. Yet, a man has his honor. Yu thought of a small falsehood; he had used it with others. He knocked the ash from his pipe.

"Many, many years ago your father loaned me a book which had the phonetic alphabet in Hangul script. It was the first I had seen. Since that day I have been indebted to your family. I will take your son to my class.

Once a week you can bring me a bundle of wood to help keep the winter chill from my old bones."

Kim saw his father moving along the darkened street. From the very way he walked, the boy knew the arrangements for school had been made. He wanted to cry out and run into the darkness before he heard the bad news. His father stood before him, gaunt and thin.

"It has been arranged, my son. You will go to the classes of Yu Jik Soo."

Kim shivered. "Yes, Father."

"The hours for your class will be from three o'clock in the afternoon until five."

Kim's heart bounded and he smiled happily. He could go to the track and still be back in time for the school.

"You will be alert and polite. The Honorable Yu is a long-time friend of your grandfather. Each seventh day you will take to him a bundle of wood. You will find the wood in the hills and along the river."

"Yes, Father—"

"More important, the police will imprison our friend if they learn he is teaching Korean. You will use the river pathway, you will move as a shadow and always go alone."

"Yes, Father, I understand."

Father Kim went inside and Kim could hear him telling his mother. Chung Soon found him in the darkness and squatted beside him.

"I was afraid you would get a morning class," she told him. "You must be careful not to be late." Chung Soon smiled, "I will find the wood for you."

Kim remembered his treasure under the seats at the track. "I will bring Schoolmaster Yu his wood."

The next morning Kim was in a panting haste to get to the track, yet he knew he must avoid the shrill-voiced woman's hutch. Her wild yelling would reveal his secret to the entire village. Though it was longer, he took a side street to avoid her and was soon past this threat. There were not many people on the road in the half-light before dawn and Kim had a heart tremor as he approached the spot where he had been accosted by the tattooed man. He began to run and the stiff morning wind in his face made it heavy labor.

Once beyond the scene of his terror, he continued at a dogtrot. His eagerness to gain the track made the distance seem long as he ran most of the way. Without pause, he slipped under the rail and crossed the track and was standing near his horse's stall when the rider came from a house nearby. Upon seeing Kim, the rider's eyebrows lifted. He said, "Good morning."

Kim stiffened and bowed, "Good morning, worthy rider of horses."

"Where do you live, Young One?"

"By the river and railroad track," Kim pointed.

"It is a long way." The rider was about to say more, but the two grooms threw open the door and led the plunging stallion from its stall. The horse was nervous, edgy and a constant care to the men holding it. The old man came from the same building from which the rider had appeared and, with the rider at his elbow, he went over the restive animal carefully. One of the grooms brought a saddle from the building and there was another outburst of rearing and plunging before it was secure. The rider settled like a feather on the horse's back and, picking up the reins, turned the animal toward the track. Kim followed just out of heel range. The ricocheting feet were kicking up puffballs of dust and gravel which the wind carried into Kim's face. He closed his eyes and moved to the right to escape the stinging dirt.

When he opened his eyes the horse was at the gate leading onto the track where the whipping wind flung a sheet of paper about its front legs. The stallion reared and swung about violently. The rider was thrown heavily against the rail and his boot caught in the stirrup. He tried desperately to swing upward and grasp the stirrup strap, but the horse whirled and the horseman struck the corner post with a crash. Then the horse began to lunge and kick at the helpless man swinging from its side. Kim cried out in terror as he charged forward. The horse swung in another horrifying circle and the reins slapped into Kim's hands. He was hurled into the air and struck the railing heavily, but clung on desperately. The frantic, savage animal pirouetted violently and Kim, like a stone in a sling, made a full circle without touching the ground.

The horse tried to run, but the weight of the boy tore cruelly at the bit and again the animal resorted to whirling.

There were shouts and the grooms ran to the scene. The horse was subdued by many hands and the old man knelt beside the stunned youth. Unaware of his rescue, Kim lay in the dirt with his hands frozen around the reins. The old trainer had to pry him loose, finger by finger. Others released the rider's foot from the stirrup and the crazed animal was led back to the stable.

The rider got slowly to his feet. He found his crop in the dust and began to slap himself clean with it. When he tried to take a step, the foot that had been locked in the stirrup buckled and muscles in his jaw rippled under the skin. Forcing himself to walk without limping, he went to where Kim sat on the ground and helped the dazed youngster to his feet. His gentle hands wiped the grime from the boy's face and brushed his clothes.

Uncontrollable tears slipped down Kim's cheeks and mixed with the dirt. The rider whispered, "You are too brave a one to cry." Kim gulped, blinked and the tears were stopped.

The old trainer said, "Are you all right, Kan?"

Kan, the rider, answered slowly, "Yes, Takeo, old friend, I am not hurt." He took a deep breath and his hand rested on Kim's head. "But for my little friend, my brains would be on every post around this track. We must look to the boy." He took Kim's hand in his and began to walk toward the stables. The boy wavered on uncertain legs and Takeo took his other hand and the three walked together.

Kim had never seen such a house as the two men took him into. There were wooden floors in every room and rich rugs and shining furniture. Takeo clapped his hands and servants came running. Kan stifled a groan as one pulled the boot from his injured leg. Inspection showed it to be swelling, but Takeo ruled that nothing serious had happened to it. Kim was told to take off his clothes and the trainer went over his body as carefully as he had the flame horse. There were many welts and bruises and Kim admitted his back was beginning to stiffen. Takeo again rendered the same verdict that he had with Kan: no serious injury.

The rider sat on a high cushion and lighted a cigarette. A servant brought a deep basin of hot water to him and he grimaced as he put his injured ankle into it. He spoke in Japanese and Kim was taken to the bathroom where the servant made him sit in a stone tub with steaming hot water to his neck. The man stood nearby and when the water began to cool, it was drained off and the tub refilled with more water near the boiling point. Kim watched his skin turn red and felt his head grow giddy. Finally the servant let him step from the tub and began to rub him so vigorously with a harsh towel Kim expected his skin to roll off his bones. When dry, the servant put salve on the open bruises. He got into his clothes and was directed into the room where Kan and Takeo waited. The rider motioned to a cushion near him while Takeo poured and handed him a cup of tea. It tasted sweet and had the fragrance of flowers. Kan smiled.

"What is your name, my friend?"

"Kim Huk Moon." Though the tea was hot, he gulped it and didn't mind the burn.

"What does your father do?"

"He works in the fields for the rice grower Miki."

"Why do you come so far to the track each day?" Kan lifted his ankle from the water and the servant refilled the basin.

"Because I dream of your red horse with the four white legs."

Takeo refilled Kim's cup. He exchanged glances with Kan and the rider nodded. The old man asked, "Would you like to work with Kan and me and our horses?"

"Oh, yes! Oh, yes!" Kim cried and the tea slopped from his cup as he began to tremble with excitement. "I would like nothing more than to lead the red horse as I saw the other boy doing."

Kan touched the top of his head. "You will be more than a lead boy. We will teach you, Takeo and I, and you will be a trainer of horses, a number one trainer."

From his purse he took a ten yen note. "It is your first month's salary as apprentice trainer to Takeo."

Kim returned the money. "I cannot work all the day. I must go to school in the afternoon. Perhaps you would let me work for less."

The two men laughed heartily and the money was forced into Kim's hand. Kan dried his foot and pulled on his boot. He stood and stamped the floor to test the ankle.

"All right, number one trainer and number two trainer, there are horses to make ready for the races, or the Honorable Colonel will be unhappy."

CHAPTER III

EXCEPT FOR THE TWO HOURS he spent each afternoon at school, life became an enchanted dream for Kim. The long walk to and from the track, the longer hours and the excitement of his new life left him drained of energy by the time he joined the other students to sit before the old scholar. There was no time to prepare his lessons and ofttimes his head nodded in sleep as the peacefulness of the classroom overcame him. Teacher Yu was unhappy with his new student and decided to speak to the father if the boy did not improve.

Each morning, as his father and mother left, Kim would hurry to the track. On arrival at the stables he would enter the house of Takeo and Kan where the servants accepted him as a special one. The old trainer and rider would be up and sipping their morning tea and Kim would breakfast with them. He was introduced to countless new dishes and for the first time in his life there were no hollows in his stomach crying for attention. His stamina improved to the point where he could dogtrot from his home to the track without tiring.

The two Japanese horsemen had taken the boy to their hearts. Kan had told him, "You were born with a love for horses. Old Takeo and I will teach you all we know about them. You will become the number one horseman in all of Chosen."

They bought Kim an outfit of clothes, even to the shiny boots and riding crop and the youngster looked like a miniature Kan when he wore them. Neither of the older men appeared to notice that the boy wore his finery only at the track and always changed into his ragged things before leaving in the afternoon.

When Kan was on the track exercising the horses, Takeo poured into Kim's ear the horse secrets he had learned in a lifetime. With meticulous care the old man drew the skeleton of a horse and each day added a muscle, a tendon or a vital organ, which Kim had to identify and explain its function. Sometimes the boy's brain groaned with the load being put on it, but his appetite to learn about horses was insatiable and he was able to absorb and retain the most meager morsel.

There were other things Kim also learned. Kan and Takeo had arrived from Japan three years previous and were in the employ of the Colonel who commanded a Japanese cavalry regiment. On one occasion Kim was presented to the Colonel and Kan recounted the tale of his courage with the raging stallion. Kim recognized the officer as the man who had given the yen note — the beginning of all his good fortune. The Colonel was a wealthy, sports-loving man who took his military post and duties lightly. Old Takeo had trained horses for the Colonel's father and Kan had been riding for the man since he was old enough to mount a horse.

There were ten race horses in the Colonel's Korean stable. These were the best of the young crop from his estate in Japan and had been brought to Korea to be kept under the eye of the Colonel and trained by Takeo. All would return to Japan for the summer race season and to escape the annual Korean deluge in July. Takeo and Kan often talked of their return to Japan and their families and considered their time in Korea as a period of exile. The thought of being parted from his friends worried Kim, but they assured him it would be some years before the Colonel was transferred. Takeo told him, "Do not spend your time borrowing trouble." It was the one piece of advice they gave that he could not completely accept.

The time of day Kim loved most was when he took Flame to the walking circle. Then it was that he and the filly were alone. Walk and walk, step and step in the circle with her sweet breath fanning his neck. When his hand rose to her head or neck, she would lean into it and when there was none to hear, he talked to her softly. It was the filly's quick acceptance of the boy that convinced Takeo and Kan he had the touch animals trust. As the two horsemen well knew, a man has such a hand at birth or he does not have it — it cannot be learned or otherwise acquired. Though he knew her name was Yuen, a Japanese word for happiness or merriment, he called her Ah-Chim-Hai and she came to respond to it. When the two men learned of the boy's name for the filly, they too began to call her by Kim's name, though they later shortened it to Flame.

Chung Soon was the only one in the family or the village who knew Kim's secret. One day she followed him to the stables and watched him walk through the area without restraint while the grooms bowed respectfully as he passed. He entered a nearby house as though he lived inside and her eyes grew to the size of saucers when she saw him come out wearing boots, riding breeches, white shirt and a red silk cap.

Chung Soon slipped away and returned home. Try as she might, she could not unravel the mystery. She knew of the bundle of wood he brought home each afternoon and of the increasing number of yen notes in the glass jar, but she could not guess at the reason for his good fortune.

Spring passed and preparations were begun to ship Flame and five other horses to Japan. The remainder of the stable would stay behind in charge of the number one groom Hirata. The trip to Japan would extend into September and they would return in time for the November race meet in Seoul. Kan asked the Colonel to allow Kim to go along, but the master ruled against the idea because he thought the boy too young.

While Kan and Takeo were gone, Kim was to come to the track each day. A servant would keep the house open and prepare food for him and he would continue to work with horses under the guidance of Hirata.

Kim accepted the news but was torn at the thought of being away from his friends. He asked, "You will bring Flame back with you?"

"Kim, my brother, do not pin your heart to a horse. Sadly, their lives are short. You will live longer than Flame or her colts or the foals of her colts."

"Please bring Flame back," the boy whispered.

"I will do all I can."

In the rush of packing and getting the horses to Inchon Harbor, Kim missed a week of school. He saw Flame into her stall on deck and whispered his good-by while she nuzzled against him. The ship sailed with Kan and Takeo waving to him from the rail. The return to the track with Hirata was a silent, lonely journey. By the time he had changed clothes and ran the two miles to his home, the evening meal was over and his father was waiting for him.

Father Kim sent the daughters outside and came directly to the point.

"Schoolmaster Yu was to see me. He says you have not been to his classes; for six days. Is that true?"

"Yes, Father."

"What have you been doing?"

Kim lowered his eyes and remained silent.

"Are you going to answer me?"

"No, Honorable Father, I cannot tell you." Kim began to tremble.

"The old lady at the five corners told me many things."

Kim burned with a sense of guilt. He put his hand in his pocket and felt the forty yen Kan had given him. He wanted to give this to his father, but hesitated. If he did, he would have to tell his secret and that would end his dream.

Father Kim considered the refusal. He sensed something deep and close to his son's heart that was keeping him silent and he fought down the anger surging through him. He sighed deeply and the cool, damp air set him to coughing. When the spasm had passed he was weak and to cover his emotions, he filled his pipe slowly, thoughtfully. His next words came haltingly.

"My son, I insist you go to Schoolmaster Yu because I do not want you to be a field worker like myself. If you learn your lessons well the Japanese will give you work in their government offices. Many invaders have come to the Land of Chosen and have been driven out. That will happen to the Japanese, too. We shall then need young men to govern our country. If you have prepared yourself, there will be a place for you when we are free again."

"Yes, Father."

"Do you say, 'Yes, Father,' because you believe my words, or because you'd like to end this talk?"

Kim remained silent.

Father Kim lighted his pipe with a coal from the stove.

"To make up for the time you have lost, I have made arrangements with Professor Yu and you'll attend his classes morning and afternoon."

It was nearly impossible for Kim to speak, but he managed to whisper, "Yes, Father."

"Now you should eat."

The next morning Chung Soon walked part way to school with Kim. She advised him, "Work hard, keep your eyes and ears open. Learn to make your figures quickly and soon you will be able to return to your horses."

The following weeks were a fever to Kim. He grew to hate the old teacher and the long hours he was forced to spend in the classroom. Knowing he would not be released from his prison until he pleased the jailer he settled to his task. His desire to be free by the time Kan and Takeo returned made a starving animal of his brain and it gobbled voraciously at all placed before it.

Only during the stillness of the night did he allow himself to think of Flame in far-off Japan. It was at night, too, that the tiger of worry clawed at him. What would Hirata think about his disappearance? The groom did not know where he lived and it would be impossible for him to come on a search. What would Kan think if he heard? These were the times when

Kim's world began to crumble and he would cry out. Chung would hear and offer the comfort of her arm until he slept.

Kim grew thin and hollow-eyed with worry and the long hours he spent over his lessons. He was always hungry now that he was missing his second breakfast and ofttimes his mouth grew wet at the thought of the food awaiting him at the house by the track.

Professor Yu sent for the father and reported remarkable progress. The teacher was more than pleased; he was enthusiastic and volunteered a long-range plan for the boy.

Kim would continue full time for another three years and then arrangements would be made to send him to a higher school conducted by a friend on the western side of Seoul Father Kim was elated by the praise and readily agreed. That evening he told the boy of his conversation with Yu and the plans that had been made. Kim felt like a trapped animal. His hard work had only gotten him into more trouble. If only Kan or Takeo were here, he would have the courage to tell his father.

Kim continued the cross-village jaunt to teacher Yu's, but the incentive was gone. The better he did, the more likely it was that he would not see Flame again and the thought burned in his mind. Overnight his work at school fell to the low standards of the early summer. Professor Yu struggled with the taciturn youngster, but there was no response. For the most part, Kim sat in the classroom with his eyes hidden behind his dreams, or he spent long hours over the drawing of the skeleton of a horse, adding to it the muscles, tendons and vital organs as Takeo had taught him.

So engrossed was he in this task one day that Yu came up behind him and observed the intricate but accurate drawing. He took it from the boy and after studying it carefully, came to a decision. The following day he turned the school over to his assistant and took the train to Sebinggo Station where he walked the half mile to the cavalry barracks. The Japanese sentry at the gate was rude and would pay no heed to him until an officer came along. It was painful for the old scholar to be so subservient, but to act otherwise would get him nothing but a hiding from the officer's riding crop. Finally he was admitted to see his old friend Chai Eyi Ja, who was second veterinarian for the Japanese cavalry unit stationed at the barracks.

It was many years since Chai and Yu had seen one another and they were drinking their second cup of tea before the horse doctor was shown Kim's sketch. He studied it for some time before looking up from the paper.

"This is an extraordinary piece of work. Who did It?"

"A young student of mine, Kim Huk Moon."

"How old is he?"

"Coming to nine in a month."

Ja looked pained. "Impossible! Your young friend has cheated. He copied it from a book." Ja rose and slipping a heavy, black book from a shelf, opened it to the desired page and placed before Yu the engraved sketch of a horse's skeleton. Gravely the schoolmaster compared one with the other as Ja peered over his shoulder.

"Do you see what I mean, old friend? The boy has a talent for drawing and copied this horse from some book."

Yu shook his head. "That could not be, respected friend. He made his drawing while in my school. No such book is available. No such picture of a horse is available in our village — of that I am certain."

"Somehow the boy has fooled you. Bring him to me and I will question him. We will have him draw another while I watch. If he can do this again, I will ask the Japanese cavalry commander to allow your young friend to become an apprentice here."

Father Kim agreed to teacher Yu's plan of taking Kim to the cavalry barracks for an examination. The following day the two traveled to the military base. The horse doctor was waiting for them at the gate and, watching Kim closely, conducted a tour of the stable area. Kim grew excited. Never before had he seen so many horses and he recognized instantly these were a type different from his Flame horse. They were larger and bigger boned than the horses at the track, but he had to admit they were fine-looking animals.

In yet another stable they came on a different type animal and Kim eyed them Intently. Doctor Ja gave the schoolmaster a covert glance.

"These horses," he said, "are used to haul the provision wagons and cannon for the cavalry when they are on maneuvers."

"These are not horses," Kim responded and was ashamed to have spoken so forthrightly.

Ja appeared not to notice the rude contradiction. "What are they, little friend, if they are not horses?"

"They are mules."

The doctor's voice became low, insistent, "What is the difference between a mule and a horse?"

Yu appeared not to be interested, but his ear was bent to the answer.

Kim realized he was getting into deep water and he was frightened of this horse doctor. This was the man who might drag his secret from him and his brain raced over the vast fields Takeo had covered with him. The answer struck him and he wanted to laugh, but restrained himself.

"A mule is a horse with a sense of humor."

Ja's eyelids fluttered in surprise and he looked at Yu and shrugged. For him this whole thing was becoming a waste of time.

He said angrily, "We will go to my quarters."

Once inside he made tea and when the cups had been filled, he placed a paper and brush on the table in front of Kim.

"The Honorable Yu tells me your fingers are very nimble. Draw me a picture of a horse such as the one you drew in school the other day."

Kim hid his eyes by sipping his tea and wished longingly that Kan and Takeo were with him.

"You will draw a horse for me, like the one you drew at the school!" The voice was harsh.

Kim began to tremble and the picture of the tattooed man flashed before his eyes. He looked at the schoolmaster and old Yu nodded in his gentle way and reached out to touch his hand. Kim sensed how much this meant to him; somehow it was important that he draw the picture of a horse. It would make teacher Yu happy and the horse doctor unhappy. Grimly, he picked up the brush. In a minute he was alone. All he knew was the picture Takeo had etched on his mind's eye. Never had his fingers been more sure or his memory more accurate. He was sweating when it was completed and he handed it to the schoolmaster, but Ja grabbed it and his long-nailed finger pointed —

"What is that?"

"Fetlock."

"And that?"

"Cannon."

"And that?"

"Poll."

"And this and this and this?" The doctor's demands were staccato.

"Pastern, quarter and crest."

"Where did you learn all this?"

Kim cast a pleading glance for help toward old Yu, but the man offered no relief. He dug his fingers into his legs and remained silent.

Doctor Ja was angered by this insolence and the breath whistled from his nostrils.

"I will take him as an apprentice-servant. That way I shall not have to go to the Japanese commander. I am allowed a servant." He turned hard eyes on Kim. "Before I teach you of horses, young friend, I will teach you manners!"

The words numbed and Kim followed the two men blindly into the courtyard. He heard from a distance the instructions the doctor was giving old Yu.

"Have his father bring him here on the seventh day to sign the papers. He will be in my charge for five years."

They were nearing the gate when a large black automobile, flags flying from fender standards, swept inside. The doctor and Yu stiffened to attention and, with eyes to the ground, bowed low. The sentry lost his overbearing manner and became a cringing first-year soldier at present arms. An officer ran from the guardhouse with soldiers sprinting behind him. The soldiers formed three frozen lines and came to attention as the officer drew his sword and saluted.

Kim's heart began to race. The man in the automobile was the Colonel! That must mean Kan and Takeo and Flame were back from Japan. He saw the polished boots approaching. They came to a stop a few feet away.

"Kan is greatly worried about you, young friend. He has gone to your house to look for you."

Kim raised his eyes. "He is back, Honorable Sir?"

The Colonel nodded and smiled. "We are off the ship just a few hours ago."

"And my Flame?"

"She misses you, she has not forgotten." The Colonel turned away and raised his voice, "Dismiss the guard." He climbed into the automobile and, as it moved away, he lifted his hand to Kim and the boy waved back.

Ja grabbed the boy. "Where did you know the Colonel? How? When? Tell me! Quickly, my little friend, dear friend. Now we can make you the number one apprentice. You will live in my quarters as a son."

Kim twisted away from the grasping hands and began to run. He didn't stop until he was at the railway station. Schoolmaster Yu arrived and they made a silent trip back to the village. Kim was waiting for the train to stop and ran from it toward his hutch. A long, gasping sigh passed his lips as he saw Kan and his father talking.

CHAPTER IV

FATHER KIM was opposed to his son working for the Japanese horseman for several reasons. Such an apprenticeship meant the youngster would be in constant contact with Japanese and his education and life would be guided by them. To a simple laborer who feared and hated the invaders of his country, nothing good could come from such an arrangement.

Furthermore, he knew nothing of horses and horse racing. It was a Japanese sport and few Koreans had the means to participate other than as onlookers, which was enough to condemn it. Also, it was impossible for Father Kim to believe Kan's interest in his son was sincere and motivated by affection.

Kan, a proud man, thought it unnecessary to explain that Kim had saved his life. How could he tell this ignorant Korean field worker a miracle had happened and horse magic had been born in his son's hands?

"I train horses for the commander of the Imperial Cavalry. It is he who has sent me to arrange that your son be an apprentice in his stables. He will be angry indeed that you have dishonored his name by not permitting your son to work for him."

Father Kim knew he was defeated. He said slowly, "My son may be an apprentice to you." He straightened his stooped shoulders. "But he should have time for school."

"Yes, I agree. That is good. The boy must learn other things besides horses. You arrange for the school in the afternoons." He took five notes from his pocket, each worth ten yen. He handed them to the father. "This is our binder. Your son will be assigned to me for five years."

It was at this point Kim came rushing along the street. Breathless from running and speechless from excitement, he threw his arms about the rider while Father Kim stared in disbelief. Suddenly he realized his son had been meeting with this Japanese for a long time — that explained what the old woman had told him. He looked at the money in his hand and tossing the bills onto the road, went into the hutch.

Kim and the rider were oblivious to all else. Kan said, "You are to be my apprentice for five years. In that time I shall be too old to ride and you can take my place while I take over from Takeo."

"I will work hard, night and day," Kim promised.

"And each afternoon you will go to school."

Kim made a face. "Do I have to?"

"I promised. Now I must return to the track. There is much to do. You come early in the morning."

"Before the sun is up," Kim laughed. Kan stepped into the waiting rickshaw and the boy stood in the street until the vehicle turned the corner and was lost to view. As he turned to go into the house, he saw the yen bills fluttering on the roadside. They were a disquieting sight and he knew sonic terrible thing had happened. Gathering the bills together, the boy went slowly into the hut. His mother was busy at the stove and did not give him her usual quick smile and Father Kim sat before the stove smoking his bamboo-stemmed pipe.

The next morning, without waiting for breakfast, Kim was on his way to the track. He raced past the shrill-voiced woman's hut, but so swiftly she failed to see him. Breathless and excited, he went directly to Flame's stall and she turned on his entrance and came to him. As he ran his hand along her neck she leaned against him and her velvet lips searched his hand for sugar. To Kim it was as though they had never been parted.

Kim was warmly greeted by the servants as he changed clothing. Then he had breakfast with Kan and Takeo and it was so much like old times he had to blink his eyes to keep the tears from slipping down his cheeks. As they ate, the horseman told him the news of the trip to Japan. Flame had pined for him at first and for a time she went off her feed. Kim was happy to hear this, but he was skeptical until Takeo assured him it was true. Flame had raced three times and had won each race with ease. Kan and Takeo laughed when they told of the money they had won from betting. The other horses had done well and the trip was a grand success, but now there was much to do to get the horses fit again after their sea trip.

The happy days sped by for Kim and there was only one cloud of worry on the horizon; his father had not spoken to him since the day Kan called, and the evening meal was a cold and silent affair.

One day many workers appeared at the track and the grounds were cleaned and the stands painted. Someone found the cache of paper and wood under the seats and it was cleaned out. This distressed Kim because he was still lugging a bundle home each afternoon on his way to school, but even this loss was forgotten in the excitement and tension of race week.

Kan explained to Kim, "The Colonel is a wealthy man and money means little to him. His love is horses. He joined the cavalry where he could be with horses. That is why Takeo and I do all we can so his horses will win. His honor is our honor."

Kim became convinced the horses felt the same way as the men and even Flame changed in those last days. The boy thought he imagined it, but as the time grew short, he was certain. No longer was she the playful, teasing animal that made being around her such fun. Racing was serious business and she knew as well as the men who trained her that the days were few.

In preparation for the meet, Kim informed schoolmaster Yu that he would be unable to attend school during this time and the old teacher accepted without objection. Since the day at the cavalry barracks he had held his horse-loving student in awe.

Kan and Takeo explained betting to the boy and how the men with the chalk and giant blackboards reached the odds on a horse. The next morning Kim brought them the glass jar and they laughed when he asked them to bet the ninety-one yen fifty sen on Flame. They cautioned him that it was not wise to place all on one bet. There was talk of a fast horse from Pusan and even Flame could lose. Kim was adamant — all on his favorite.

One morning it was as though flood gates had been opened and a torrent of people let loose. They packed the stands, the center-field area, and hung over the rails. Some had drunk too much sul and were boisterous and noisy as crowds gathered around the sweating men making figures on the blackboards. Kim resented the invasion of the quiet, idyllic life he had grown to love and it was evident that Takeo felt much the same way as he muttered, "Man takes a drink, the drink takes a drink, the drink takes the man."

Then all was forgotten save the preparation, of their charges to run their best. There were to be four races in the morning and eight in the afternoon. The morning races were unimportant and none of the Colonel's stable raced in them. In the afternoon Flame was to run in the feature race, which was named in honor of the Japanese Governor-General. The purse was for a thousand yen and a large gold cup.

As Kan explained to Kim, "The money is nothing, but the cup is important. We have won it twice; If we win it this time, the Colonel can keep it."

Kim told his friend, "No horse can beat Flame."

"You're wrong, little trainer. Loyalty is fine, but don't let it blind you. There are over a thousand ways for a horse to lose a race. That is why you will always find people who will bet on other horses, though Flame is a winner in Japan. That is why I am sweating on a cool day!" He smiled, "And now it is time we dress for the race."

In the house Kim found a new outfit of clothing Kan and Takeo had bought for him in Tokyo. The shirt was of Rising Sun red with the Colonel's family crest in white on the back. The riding breeches were white and snug at the knees and the boots were black and shiny. Kan and Takeo were pleased with the boy's delight and the old trainer said, "One day I hope to give you a hand up on a horse I've trained."

By the time Flame was to be led to the paddock for the parade and saddling, Kim's teeth were chattering. He pulled his long-visored cap low over his eyes, and taking the lead strap in hand he began to walk Flame along the outside rail of the track. The filly was restive, excited and small flecks of foam spattered from her mouth. Without looking at her, Kim was aware of the change. It came into his hands through the lead strap and was as definite as an electric impulse.

The Colonel was waiting with a party of friends and Kim went directly to the group. The officer was pleased with Kim's new clothing and told the story of how he had saved Kan's life. The boy was embarrassed and relieved when Takeo motioned to begin walking Flame around the paddock. Then it was time for the saddling and Takeo lifted Kan up on the horse.

The rider smiled down on them. "Do not worry too much, my friends, we will not disgrace you."

Takeo and Kim went to the place near the finish line reserved for trainers and grooms. The old trainer pointed out the merits and faults of the other five horses in the race. He dismissed three curtly.

"Their owners have more money than sense. They are willing to pay for the honor of saying their horses ran in the Governor-General Cup Race." Takeo never took his eyes from the horses on the track as he talked. "They will also be invited to the exalted Governor's home for food and drink tonight. That is important to some people. We can only hope those three cart horses don't clutter the track and prevent an honest race."

He directed Kim's attention to the chestnut horse leading the parade. "Look closely at the stallion from Pusan. He is all horse and will give Flame all the run she can handle, I fear. With him starting on the inside and our little one on the outside, it may be too much for her. At sixteen hundred meters he will finish strong."

"Do you really think she may lose, Honorable Takeo?"

"But for Kan, I would sit this race out in the darkness of a stall. Watch him closely, Little One. He is part horse and his hands talk horse-talk. A horse will run faster than it can run, because of Kan. It is he who has made me the number one trainer."

There was a hush in the crowd as the six horses formed a line abreast and walked toward the starting line. Flame was on the outside with the three cart horses inside and then came a fractious bay from Taegu and the stallion from Pusan in the favored position. The walk-up was not orderly nor even and the starter sent them back for another try. Once more the six walked to the line. Just as they neared the tense moment of starting, the cart horse next to Flame reared and swung its hindquarters in her direction. Fearful of a kick, Kan spun his mount away. At that moment the starter shouted, "Go!"

The crowd roared in dismay and old Takeo beat his hands on the railing. "The man is blind! A blind fool, he is!"

Kim wanted to throw himself to the ground and hide his eyes and close his ears. Yet he could do neither as his eyes glued themselves to the horses speeding down the track. Head and head and running at a terrific pace were the Pusan stallion and the Taegu gelding. Strung behind them loosely like badly strung pearls were the three cart horses and far behind came Flame with Kan nestled over her neck.

"Ten lengths behind. It is too much!" Takeo muttered and Kim threw him a shocked glance. When the boy looked back to the race the horses were entering the first turn and Flame had ranged alongside the rearmost cart horse. Slowly, slowly, foot by foot, she edged by and gained on the next in line. Around the turn and into the back stretch the two leaders sped as though death was at their heels with Pusan holding a lead of inches on Taegu.

At the eight-hundred-meter pole Flame was by the second cart horse and at the withers of the third. There was open daylight of sixty feet between her and the two leaders. Takeo took in the situation at a glance and looked to the instruction of his pupil.

"The Taegu horse is not bred for such a pace. He will begin to quit on the far turn. This Kan knows, but to save ground he must come through on the inside. And then the race rests in his hands and Flame's heart —"

To keep his teeth from chattering, Kim clenched them and spoke through taut lips, "Is there a chance?"

Takeo squinted and his face lightened as he saw something that pleased him. Over the bedlam of the crowd he shouted in Kim's ear, "There is one, if Kan sees—"

As though he had used a divining rod, Takeo's prophecy came true and the Taegu horse wilted suddenly; spirit, strength and heart left it at the same time. Flame was past the last cart horse and slipping up on the inside of the faltering Taegu. In a breathless instant she was by this threat and creeping in on the flying Pusan. The crowd let out a full-throated roar as the daylight between the two shrank to less than thirty feet.

The stallion raced into the final turn with Flame closing on his heels. The rider cast a hurried glance over his shoulder and, seeing Kan bearing down on him, began to whip his mount. The chestnut came around the last turn with the rider's arm flailing and slowly a handbreadth of distance showed between the stallion and the inside rail. Then it was three, then four and five hands as he bore out; then Flame was in that space and running hard. Kim gasped as he saw her head-on; he could hardly recognize his playful, gentle stable pet. This was a different animal, with eyes burning and every muscle and tendon strained to outrace the horse at her side,

Takeo shouted in his ear, "It is all over, Little One. Go to the winner's circle!"

A hundred meters from the finish Flame was in the lead by half the length of her neck and Kan's splendid hands gave her the strength to hold her advantage. On legs weak as bamboo sprouts, Kim ran along the track to meet them as the filly came back at a rocking horse gallop, her head nodding to the thunderous plaudits of the crowd. When she came to Kim she forgot her vanity and rubbed her sweat-wet head against him and he told her she had done well Kan leaned over and laughed, "Remember! I told you there are a thousand ways to lose a race."

Takeo was waiting for them at the winner's circle and for a moment only the four of them were together. The rider laughed and winked and Takeo nodded and between them Kim sensed a secret.

The presentation of the Governor-General's Cup was a tiresome, wordy affair and Takeo fretted that Flame would take a chill before a blanket could be placed on her. Finally it was over and Kim led her back to the stable and all along the way people shouted and cheered.

It was always a joy to walk Flame in the cooling circle, but today it was pure ecstasy. After she was cool he loitered over the rubbing of her legs and as her racing fever subsided she became the pet he knew best.

Hirata came from the betting ring with the winnings and Kim stared at the two hundred ten yen that was his share. Kan asked him, "What are you going to do with so much money? Bet it on other races and bankrupt the moneyman?"

Kim shook his head, "I'll not bet again. I might lose and if I did, I'd never be able to buy my dream."

"What do you dream, little Kim Huk Moon?"

"Of owning Flame—"

The rider stilled his impulse to laugh and said soberly, "It is a good dream."

Over late afternoon tea Kim learned the secret between his two friends. The telling of it added another upright to his storehouse of knowledge of horses and racing.

Old Takeo said, "Remember when I told you there was one chance for Kan and Flame?"

The boy nodded.

"It was then I noticed the Pusan horse was leading with his right front leg. If he went into the last turn without changing leads, he would bear out and leave an opening for Kan." Kan leaned forward, his eyes lively with good humor. "That is why I stayed on the rail. Flame had not enough strength left to go around and win. When Yang began to whip with his right hand, I knew the right lead and whip would drive the horse away from the rail enough for us to get through."

Kim was dismayed. How could he ever learn all there was to know about horses and racing? He stayed late that night listening to the men talk. The excitement of the race loosened their tongues and story after story came his way. It was dark when he stopped by Flame's stall and she turned eagerly and nickered on his entrance. The nervousness of racing was gone entirely and she began nibbling at his pocket for sugar.

On the road for home Kim broke into his easy swinging dogtrot. There was no moon and his pace quickened as he neared the spot where he had been accosted by the tattooed man. He welcomed the sprinkling of huts at the edge of the village and slackened his pace to a fast walk because of the Japanese police.

"And now you prowl at night, Kim Huk Moon!" the shrill voice shrieked and Kim nearly jumped from his rubber shoes in surprise. Did the old woman never sleep? He ducked into an alley to avoid any police alerted by her yelping. He was wet from sweat and panting when he stepped from his shoes and crept into his hutch. Scarcely breathing, he made his way into the backyard and bathed at the earthen bowl, knowing it had been left full for him by Chung Soon. He dried himself and, retrieving the money from his clothes, crept onto the sleeping pad. He was so tired even the bones in his legs felt limp. Tucking the money under the sleeping pad, he yawned widely and was asleep.

It was late fall when the race meet was over and the Colonel's stable moved to the cavalry barracks where Kim was to learn the training of cavalry horses in jumping, movement in formation and facing up to cross-country obstacles. As the weeks slipped into months and winter passed, there was no worry in his life save the strain when he was with his father. Since the day Kan had come to the hutch, Father Kim had not spoken to the boy and Mother Kim suffered for him, but could understand her husband and his hurt. When Father Kim was taken to bed with a severe cold and there was no money coming in from the fields, Kim emptied the glass jar into his mother's hands. She used of it sparingly and told her husband the money came from what she had hoarded. He did not believe her, but was too ill to protest. After three weeks he returned to the fields, more gaunt and bent than ever.

The following spring Takeo gave Kim a hand-up to his first horse and he started riding lessons under Kan's critical eye. Weeks later, he rode Flame on a gallop around the track and felt he had reached a crest in his life that would not be surpassed. After a time, he became exercise boy to the number two horses trained for sale.

The trip to Japan that summer showed Kim sights his wildest dreams could not match. He bought presents for the family at the huge stores in Tokyo and when he returned home he no longer changed into his ragged clothing. When he arrived at the mud and wattle hutch Nam Soon was home alone, Chung Soon now being old enough to work in the fields. She was delighted with the dress goods he brought her and promised to have the most beautiful dress in the village. Kim felt it might be easier for his father to accept presents if he were not in the house when they came in from the fields. So he left Nam Soon measuring and planning her dress and walked slowly along the road toward the five street intersection to deliver his present to Schoolmaster Yu.

The Japanese officer eyed him suspiciously and shouted, "Come here, you!" The black, polished stick hanging from his wrist looked ugly and menacing.

"Who are you?"

"Kim Huk Moon."

"What have you in your hand?"

"A present for a friend."

The policeman tore it from Kim's hand and ripped the paper from the tin of Japanese tea.

"Where did you steal this?"

"I bought it in Japan."

"In Japan! You are a liar as well as a thief." He slapped Kim across the mouth. "Come." Grasping the boy by the collar and shouting at the crowd to disperse, the officer marched his prisoner across the street and into the police station.

"I have a thief," he announced grandly to the sergeant. "He has a pound tin of tea he says he bought in Japan."

Kim looked at the senior officer and said, "I am Kim Huk Moon, apprentice horseman. I live at the cavalry barracks with tie great rider Kan and the number one trainer Takeo. We have just returned from racing in Japan where I bought the tea."

The hand on Kim's collar went limp and fell away. The sergeant glared at the first-year policeman. "Give the boy his tea." The sergeant drew in a deep breath between his teeth and his round, moon face creased into a forced smile. "An unfortunate mistake. Please pay my respects to your Honorable Colonel and tell him we consider you the most honored Korean in our village."

For two squares down the street Kim could hear the sergeant shouting at the dejected first-year policeman. He bowed low to the old woman who did not recognize him in his new clothes. She stared and stared and he was half a square away before it came to her who had passed by her door. She was too dumbfounded to find voice and sat brooding in silence.

At the school he found the old teacher with his back to the west so as to catch the last rays of warmth from the setting run. He turned his faded eyes from the Han River and spoke a warm greeting as Kim held out the tin of tea. The old man took it and read the characters with care.

He said, "I know nothing of the life of men who race horses. It seems a futile, worthless existence. Are you satisfied with your choice?"

"Oh, yes, yes, Honorable Yu! I want nothing else but to live with my horse."

"There is so little happiness in this Land of Chosen I cannot condemn you for a wastrel life with the Japanese."

Kim looked at the ground. "Will you speak to my Honorable Father? He has said no word to me since I became an apprentice."

"Counsel makers between father and son are repulsed like iron on iron. It is for you to find a way back into his heart. Remember, they killed his father — your grandfather."

Kim turned sadly away. A short distance down the pathway Yu's voice halted him. "You have a good heart, little Kim Huk Moon, and your present has brought joy to an old man."

It was dark when Kim entered his home. The aroma of Japanese tea mixed with that of tobacco told him his father had accepted the presents. His mother and Chung Soon greeted him with warm, happy arms and there was unrestrained chattering over the gifts he had brought them. Although Father Kim did not speak, there was a new warmth to his eyes as he gazed on his son.

The wheel of time spun slowly. There were more race meets and more traveling. At the request of the Governor-General, Flame was taken to the races at Pusan and Taegu. The other horses under the charge of Kan and Takeo were tried and those found wanting were sold. The better ones were saved and shipped to Japan for breeding while Flame stayed on because she was the favorite of all. Now that Kim was more skilled and experienced in riding, he exercised her every morning and the attachment and understanding between the two deepened until it became a mysterious, psychic element transcending human or animal links. The old trainer and Kan had watched this strange growth from the first day the boy had touched the little mare. They could not explain it, but they knew such things happened and did not question or hinder.

They still talked of the winter's night when they were in quarters at the cavalry barracks seated around the charcoal brazier. Kan was mending a saddle, Takeo was smoking and dreaming and Kim was making good his promise to study characters an hour each day. The boy's head had jerked up and his eyes carried a startled, fearful expression. He jumped to his feet and ran to the door.

"Flame needs me," he said as he raced away in the darkness. They followed close behind and in the large box stall they found the white-stockinged mare cast in a position that would have done injury to her had she struggled.

One day Kan and Takeo asked the boy to join them in their room overlooking the barracks stables. Both were serious and more formal than usual.

Kan spoke, "Little brother, your apprenticeship is over. This is your birthday. Five years ago this day you saved my life. What is your wish? Do you want us to find a place for you in another stable?"

"Oh, no, Kan, no!" Kim cried. "I never want to leave you and Takeo. I would die to leave Flame. Let me stay, let nothing change."

Old Takeo shook his head. He was feeling his age this day and was more weary than usual. "We will do what we can for you, little friend, but life is constant change and nothing remains still."

Kan placed his hand on the boy's shoulder. "We have spoken to the Colonel. You will become number two trainer in the stable. You will ride second horses in the morning races."

"In Japan, too?" Kim asked.

Kan sobered. "I don't know. A war has started in Europe. We may not go to Japan until it is over."

Takeo spoke slowly. "Wars are like glanders in a stable. They spread slowly and kill many; there is no explaining them. Life is uncertain in peacetime, but in wartime, never look beyond the next minute."

CHAPTER V

TAKEO BECAME ILL during the winter. He was put to bed in the barracks infirmary, but he grew worse and the Colonel ordered him taken to the Medical College Hospital. He drove to the place to see that the old man was properly quartered and the doctors made aware of his importance. Kan and Kim made the trip with their friend and saw him safely to bed.

On the way back Kan told the boy, "If there is racing next season, you will do most of the riding. It is time I climbed down from the saddle."

"Don't you think Takeo will get well?"

"He is an old man. This illness will make him older. When he is well enough to leave the hospital he will be sent back to Japan to retire. Then it will be you and I to take care of the horses."

After many weeks, Takeo was released from the hospital. The rider and Kim went for him and helped pack his few belongings and walked down the long corridors that were enveloped in the odor of medicine. The boy was distressed by the change in his friend. It was as though all the years had rolled up and struck him a mighty blow on the shoulders.

In the Colonel's black military automobile they drove the convalescent to the barracks where he spent the night with them. In the morning he made the rounds of the stable and said goodbye to the grooms and horses. In Flame's stall he broke down and cried and hid his face in her mane.

Later they saw him to his cabin aboard the ship at Inchon. From somewhere he drew on a secret supply of strength and squared his shoulders.

"I will meet you in Japan soon and we will race together once more, the three of us. We were a great team. We filled the Colonel's trophy case with cups. We will do it again."

Kim wanted to cry as he held the old man close and felt the sharp bones and smelled the age of him. The rider was equally disturbed and the automobile was on the outskirts of Sosa before either found words.

Kim spoke first, "Being at home with his family will do him good. Maybe he will get strong enough to work again?"

Kan shook his head. "The days of his years are numbered. All we can do is pray they will be easy ones."

"And you will be number one trainer and rider."

"You will be number one rider." At the boy's startled expression Kan hurried on, "I have spoken to the Colonel. I am too old to ride."

"But you are not old," Kim protested.

Kan agreed smilingly, "As a man, that is true. As a rider, it is not. With horses you have always been old beyond your years. You are fourteen, you will be the number one rider."

"And I will ride Flame in a race!" Kim cried.

"You will ride Flame in her last race — this is her last season. If she were not such a great one and a favorite of all, she would even now be on the big place in Japan raising colts for us to train and race."

Kim dug his toes into the rich nap of the carpeting in the automobile. When she retired someone else would be caring for her; he might never see her again. He whispered, "Since the first day I saw her I've dreamed of owning her."

"I know. Your heart is in your eyes." Then, softly, "It can never be, number one, so don't build your castles. The Colonel would not sell her for all the gold in the Imperial Treasury."

Since the completion of his apprenticeship, it was Kim's custom to spend one night a week with his family. He would take the train from Sebinggo Station to the village, where it was a fifteen-minute walk to his home. Along the way he saw many old friends and reminders of the days he ran the dusty streets — even the old woman, looking like a mummy in rags, still shrilled at him though her voice did not carry as it once did. The first-year policeman at the five-street intersection was now a veteran policeman who glared in remembrance of the day he lost face.

Nam Soon had married and was living with her husband in the village of Kumho-Dong. Her man was a worker for a silk manufacturer and spent his days tending the vast fields of mulberry. Chung Soon, though older than her sister, had shunned marriage and it was a sore point with her parents.

With each visit, Kim was shocked by the hunched, sickly look of his father, whose cough was worse — after a bad spell he hid the cloth that had been to his lips. Chung Soon confirmed what he suspected. The father's health was such that he was now missing two days' work in seven, but, even worse, Mother Kim had begun to cough.

"What can I do?" Kim asked. "I have more than five hundred yen in the Bank of Chosen."

Chung shook her head sadly. "Father accepts your food because a hungry stomach knows no pride, but he would not accept your help to a Japanese hospital."

"The second doctor at the barracks is a Korean. I will ask him to come to see Father."

Dr. Yik made the trip to the village and when he returned, his expression was grave.

"Your father has tuberculosis in the advanced stage."

"And my mother?"

"She is a more recent victim."

"What can I do?"

"Nothing," Dr. Yik said bitterly. "The disease is the curse of our land. Overwork, too little rice and cold, drafty houses will, in time, destroy our people. All you can do is make their lives easier while they live. I will give you a medicine that will ease the coughing and induce sleep."

Kim took the medicine to his home the next day and for the first time in six years spoke directly to his father and urged him to stop work and sit in the sun and rest. The old man heard him out and, turning on his heel, left the room. Kim knew he was defeated; he left the medicine with Chung Soon and returned to the barracks.

Kim lost himself in his work. Each day there were ten horses to exercise and his body grew lean and tough and his mind alert and senses tuned to the spirit of the animal between his knees. With all horses he instinctively sensed their vagaries, but with Flame there was more — it was as though they spoke a language unknown to others.

Kan watched the boy develop into an excellent rider and once a month the two wrote Takeo a long letter. As Kan said, "This contact will keep his heart alive."

As the time grew near for the race meet, Kim felt wires of tension turning tighter and tighter inside himself. No longer did he sleep the calm, dreamless sleep of the unworried as night after night he awakened to find himself sitting stiffly upright and sweating. Flame had fallen and broken a leg; Flame had been crowded into the rail and a shaft of wood had run her through; Flame had been crippled by a kicking stallion. Each time the dream was different, but each was tragic, each ended with a pistol shot in her brain.

Kan sensed the disquiet in the boy and saw it in the pale, taut face and a doubt flickered through him. Was it possible there was a flaw and the boy could not face up to racing competition? Was he a morning rider, an exercise boy only?

Kan watched in silence and when he handed the boy into the saddle for a second-class morning race, he covered his misgivings with a confident smile.

"Make your first race a winning one."

Kim's horse was to start in the middle of a large field of nine. It was for horses who had never won five races and no whips or spurs were allowed. Most of the horses were young, frisky and not well trained, making the minutes at the starting line a jostling, bucking turmoil. At the starter's shout the pack broke in a melee. There were horses on Kim's right and left and there were horses in front of him and others running up on his heels. He held his position coolly and when daylight showed between the horses ahead of him, he steered his mount into it. Then he was through and clear save for the two horses running as a team ahead of him.

His hands told him his horse was running at its limit and he eased it back. Riding easily and nursing his horse along the rail, Kim followed three lengths behind the pair in front. His horse had only one short burst of speed left and he waited for the moment to use it. Patiently he followed the length of the backstretch into the far turn. As the leaders swung into the long drive for home a breath of light shone on the rail and Kim threw his mount into it. His right foot hit the rail and his left knee cracked that of his rival, but he slipped through.

There were still two hundred meters to run when he had gained the lead by a long neck, but his mount was done. In his hands and knees Kim felt the flagging strength of the horse and to give it new heart and confidence, he eased it back a touch. Inch by inch the other horse gained until they were as even as horses in tandem could be. Kim waited until they were twenty meters from the finish when he gently, surely mustered his horse for a final effort.

"Now!" he yelled and the horse responded. Kim rose in the stirrups and eased his mount. He knew he had won by a nose.

At the winners' circle Kan was waiting and as he gave Kim a hand down he whispered, "You'll make an old man of me."

Though Kim rode three other races, he was in a state of funk by the time it came to ride Flame in the feature race. His face was pale, his hands shook and sweat streamed from every pore.

"Are you sick?" Kan asked sharply,

"No—"

"Are you afraid?"

"Yes," Kim whispered. He saw the expression on Kan's face and knew his friend had misunderstood. "Not for myself, but I'm afraid for Flame. Night after night I have dreamed that she has been hurt, that we have had to shoot her. I don't want her to race."

Kan guided him into Flame's stall. "Look at her," he directed. "She was bred for racing, it is her life. If she is to get hurt, she will accept the bullet as a man of honor accepts the harakiri blade. Flame loves two things, you and racing. And on race day she loves racing more than she does you." Kan stroked her neck. "She will need your help to carry the hundred fifty-nine pounds they've loaded on her. One day they break her heart with iron."

In the paddock Kim took a hand-up from Kan and as he settled in the saddle Flame headed for the track. As though in a fog the boy went through the parade before the stands and the walk-up to the starting line. The, little red mare kept her position so that none gained an advantage; no horse could crowd her and prove a hamper, and all the time she awaited the shout of the starter. When it came she was away like a shot and in less than a hundred meters she was clear of the pack and ranged alongside the horse on the rail. Stride for stride, the two raced into the turn and on around. The excitement of the race caught Kim and he forgot his fears. He exulted in the confidence and speed of the little horse under him, yet the horse on the rail clung to its lead of a neck and matched Flame, stride for stride. In this fashion they sped the length of the long sweep of backstretch and into the turn for the finish line.

Kim felt Flame begin to gather for the long run home. She moved up on her rival and was in the lead by the length of her neck when she seemed to hang in midstride. Flutterings of anxiety came along the reins and into Kim's hands as she frantically called on him for help. Kim looked down and back to see the rival rider, crouching low, hanging onto Flame's saddle cloth. Kim lashed out with his whip, striking the fellow's wrist a cutting blow and Flame shot into the lead.

The crowd roared as their favorite sped under the wire fifty meters in the lead. Flame came back to the winner's circle in her arched-neck, rocking horse gallop and tossing her head to the cheering people. All the way back to the stable she tossed her head and minced along on primping steps until Kim laughed at her vanity.

"I was a help to you," he told her. "You didn't win it all by yourself, you know."

One night, not long after, a soldier-orderly awakened Kan at midnight and told him he was wanted by the Colonel. Kan dressed hurriedly and left. When he' returned he sat on a folded blanket beside Kim's sleeping pad.

"War has started between Japan and the United States. Already there has been a big battle and we have won."

Kim held his breath as he tried to imagine what a battle was like. He had seen the cavalry in their parade ground exercises and supposed it was like these maneuvers.

He asked, "What will happen to the Colonel?"

"He leaves tomorrow. He will take an airplane from Kimpo and I go with him."

Kim tried not to let Kan hear the heavy sigh, "Let me go with you?"

Kan took his hand. "No, Little One. Overnight you are to become the Big One. All the cavalry horses will soon be shipped to Japan. Until arrangements can be made to ship Flame and the others to Japan, you'll take them to the track stables and care for them until word comes. Hirata will be instructed that you are the number one."

"What will you do?"

"Fight for the Emperor, of course. If we all fight with the spirit of the Yamato race, no one can resist us. I have often thought that flying an airplane must be like riding a horse over the jumps. The Colonel will arrange that I go into training to become a war flyer." He smiled, "I will take a flying machine jumping over the clouds rather than a horse over the ground."

Kim saw his friends off from the Kimpo Airport. It was a sad parting and he stood on the flight apron for a long time after the plane was out of sight. Throughout the long ride from Kiinpo, through Yongdongpo and across the Han River he sat in the black military automobile staring from the window without seeing a thing along the way. At the track he went to Flame's stall, put his arm around her neck and pressed his face into her mane.

The days and weeks rolled by with little change. The horses were exercised, cared for and put back into their stalls. The government announced there would be no more racing until the war was over, and the other horses housed at the track were taken away until only the Colonel's ten remained.

The coming of the war had made other changes which Kim noted. The people in the fields worked longer hours and fewer gasoline driven vehicles were seen on the road to Yongdongpo and Inchon. After a time, some of the trucks reappeared with huge, smoke-belching tanks on the rear and Hirata explained that the machines now ran on charcoal.

Kim and his group were left alone and there was no curtailment of rice and other foods for them, but as increasing quantities of rice were shipped to Japan, there was less and less for Koreans. Chung Soon told Kim about the strict rationing and he increased the amount he took the family on his weekly visits.

After a long time, a letter arrived from Kan stating he was happy with flying and was now taking his plane up alone. He sent along a snapshot, which didn't look at all like the man Kim remembered. The letter also told him Takeo was still hanging onto life and that the Colonel was out of the country fighting for the Emperor.

Each night Kim would read the Korean Times along with Hirata and the other grooms — there was nothing but victory for the imperial forces of the Emperor. At each reading the Japanese would grow excited and shout, "Genno Heika, Banzai!" Kim wondered what had happened to the plan of shipping the horses to Japan.

One night he went home to find his mother completely unnerved and wailing; Father Kim had been drafted by the police and shipped away to work on a dam in the Hwachon area. The village was to supply one hundred men for the project and Father Kim's name had been drawn by lot from the files at the police station. That he was a sick man and no longer capable of hard work had not the slightest effect on the police sergeant. The police had arrived in the middle of the night and before daylight the enforced laborers were aboard a train and jolting northward.

Kim went to the police station, but knew it was hopeless when he saw that the man in charge was the Japanese who had been reprimanded for falsely accusing him of theft. His hard eyes studied Kim.

"And what are you doing to help the war effort?" he asked as his dirty fingers ruffled through a file of papers and came out with one bearing Kim's name.

"I work for His Excellency the Colonel, as I always have."

"We will see, we will see," the policeman said. He took his brush and wrote on the card. "Now, get out of here. You waste my time."

Kim did his best to console his mother before taking the train to the cavalry barracks station where he would appeal to one of the officers who knew him. This proved a fruitless trip for there had been a complete change-over in personnel and he could not even gain entrance to the grounds. Upon his return to the track he found the horses and stablemen being mustered by a Japanese in army uniform with a long sword clattering at his heels.

Kim bowed low before the man. "I am Kim Huk Moon, number one rider for His Excellency the Colonel. These horses were left in my charge, Honorable Sir. May I ask what you propose to do with them?"

The officer looked at Hirata. "Does this Korean speak the truth?"

"Yes, Honored One. Trainer Kim is much esteemed by our most worthy Colonel."

The officer ignored Kim and spoke to Hirata, "You will take your horses to the farms south of Inchon. You and the animals will work the fields and haul rice to the ships in Inchon harbor."

To Kim the proposal was so utterly without reason it took some time before it penetrated. He thought of Kan and the Colonel and what they would say when they learned Flame and the others were cart horses. A groan escaped him at the thought of Flame hauling heavy loads over the rough roads.

"His Excellency, the Colonel, ordered me to keep his horses here until he sent for them. We are to go to Japan soon. Therefore, Most Worthy One, I cannot do what you order."

The officer's face went red and his hand flashed out to strike the boy across the mouth. "Keep your insolent words to yourself." He turned to Hirata. "What is your name?"

"Jiro Hirata, sir."

"You will be in charge. Put this Korean dog to work as a servant." Hirata bowed and the Japanese officer struck a pose. "Our enemies, the Yankee big noses, are strong. All must work to bring victory to the Emperor." He was being carried away by his own oratory — "Face the east. You too, Korean dog! Worship the Imperial Palace! The supreme salute!" They bowed in silence.

After the time of reverence had been observed, the man spoke again, "It is the will of his Excellency, the Governor-General, that these horses work for the Emperor." He strode away with the sword scabbard fingering a thin line in the dust. As though he had forgotten until this moment, he turned and there was a cruel smile on his lips.

"Your Colonel is dead. He fought well and died for the Emperor. He fell like a cherry blossom."

Kim was awakened from his shock by Hirata ordering, "Put the horses back into their stalls. We will depart at first light in the morning. Be packed and ready."

The boy looked at the groom. Hirata met his gaze and his eyes were unfriendly.

"I am in charge now. The officer said so. I will move into the house and you will move into the stable. You will care for —" He was on the point of assigning the mare to another when he thought better of it, "You will care for Flame." And then, to impress the others, "I will be watching to see that you do it right."

Kim bundled his riding clothes together and took them home, explaining to Chung Soon and his mother that he would be unable to see them as often as he had before. There had been no word from Father Kim since his departure for Hwachon. Schoolmaster Yu had sent off a letter of inquiry to a former student who was working as a draftsman on the project. Mail between Koreans was slow and indifferent. It might be weeks or never. He left money and promised to return when possible.

Kim was surprised but not too disappointed over the change in Hirata. All would be corrected when the war ended and Kan returned and he resolved not to get into trouble with the groom. As long as he could be with Flame, little else mattered.

The journey to the south was begun before daylight and it was slow going. The grooms were clumsy in affixing the packs of personal belongings to the horses, and the animals were restive under the strangeness of this new activity. Flame's vanity suffered a cruel blow and she reached an emotional point where she would have bucked her way from under her undignified load had Kim not soft-talked her into being good. It was a sad day for the grooms and the horses to leave the track and the scene of so many triumphs. Even Hirata, who had garnered himself a long walking stick as a symbol of his new authority, felt it.

The cavalcade went south. As they passed the commercial school the students who were in the yard washing their rice bowls, stared at them. Farther along the way the chemical plant was spewing out a stench-heavy white smoke and the horses snuffled and the grooms breathed through nose rags. At the gate leading into the cavalry barracks the horses strained against lead ropes and were further disheartened when forced to go on.

While they all waited for the ferry at the Sobinggo crossing, Kim went to a nearby shrine. He gave the Buddhist monk fifty sen and wrote a prayer for the Colonel and fastened it to the prayer wheel. With Flame standing beside him, he knelt and prayed for his father's health and safe return. The shouts of Hirata and the others intruded upon the quiet of the morning and he and the mare hurried back to the ferry.

All through the day they walked along the dusty roads to the south and it was dark when they reached their destination. They were shown a small hutch in which to sleep, but there were no stables for the horses. Grumbling and stumbling about in the darkness, the horses were off-loaded and the packs opened. Kim gave Flame an extra portion of barley and rubbed her down thoroughly. She was through eating before he was satisfied with her condition. Blanketing her, he led her into a vacant end of the hut.

The others had built a fire in the stove and were drinking tea while waiting for their rice to cook. Hirata watched the boy clear a space for Flame, his face screwed into a look of disapproval.

"Put her outside with the rest."

Kim chose his words carefully. "As long as there is room, Flame should be inside. We must keep her in good health and condition for our Honorable Kan. It is the least we can do for our friend." Then he added with emphasis, "When I rode to the flying field with his Excellency the Colonel and the Honorable Kan, the last words they spoke were of Flame's welfare."

All were impressed and Hirata was forced to agree.

In the morning they discovered their hutch was near a high enclosure of barbed wire. Inside the wire compound were many men, giants of men. A Japanese official told them they were American prisoners — big noses from America who had been defeated and captured by the victorious soldiers of the Emperor.

"Big noses have no honor," he told them. "They allow themselves to be captured. They know nothing of the soul of the soldier."

The rules of conduct and their duties were kid down. Japanese soldiers would guard and control the prisoners both inside the wire compound and while working the fields. Hirata and his group would take instructions from the supervisor of the farms and haul rice and other farm produce to Inchon for shipment overseas. Stern measures would be taken with anyone fraternizing with the prisoners.

Flame accepted the harness and shafts of the cart with resignation. Kim tried to explain matters to her, but was sure her expression was one of reproach and disgust. In the fields he came close to the white foreigners and it was plain to see why they were called big noses. Kim marveled at the size of them — tall and straight like bamboo, but they all looked alike. There was one, however, he could distinguish from the others because his hair was so yellow, his eyes so blue.

The blond's appraisal of Flame was experienced and admiring.

"That's quite a horse you've got there, Buster."

Kim had never heard such a soft, drawling voice. It made him think of slow water over a gentle spillway. He wished he understood the words. The prisoner put his hand on Flame's neck and she leaned into it. For Flame to react in such manner to a stranger was most unusual. Kim smiled.

Speaking in halting Japanese, the man asked, "Are you Nipponese?"

Kim shook his head vigorously, "I am Korean." He picked up a handful of earth to show he was from the Land of Chosen. "I am Kim Huk Moon."

"Kim Huk Moon —" The giant pointed a long finger at himself, "Bill Duffy."

"Bill Duffy," Kim repeated the words slowly.

A Japanese soldier saw them and came running with his bayonet at thrust position. A Japanese officer heard and he, too, came running. With one swipe Kim was struck to the ground. While the soldier held Duffy at bayonet point, the officer beat the American over the head and shoulders with a leather riding crop. The tall man took the beating without change of expression while other prisoners watched in bitter silence.

After the officer tired, the giant was led away to the monkey cage for punishment while the others were hustled to loading the carts. Hirata shouted and waved his arms to impress the officer and Kim was warned — if he were seen talking to another big nose he would be sent north to work in the mines.

The trip to Inchon was long and hot. The cart was unevenly loaded and the harness was too large and wore into Flame's tender hide. Kim did all he could to ease her torment by tearing his shirt into shreds and wrapping pieces about the leather digging into her. By constant care and attention no open sores developed. The other horses did not fare so well as the grooms would not sacrifice clothing to protect their charges, but Hirata seemed oblivious to all save his new position of leader as he strutted in front, waving a large bamboo walking staff.

There were more prisoners on the Inchon docks and they unloaded the carts. A long wait ensued as Hirata and his ten carts were forced to wait in a lengthy queue and darkness came before they were back in the hutch alongside the barbed wire enclosure. Kim mixed Flame an extra ration of grain, and while she ate he rubbed her vigorously, working an ointment into the spots worn by the harness. After blanketing her, he spent an hour massaging her legs and caring for her feet — and worried about a crack developing in her quarter.

When he went to the stove for food there was nothing left but cold soya bean soup. In silence Kim built up the fire and heated the soup, but it was so thin it did nothing for the drawstrings of hunger pain in his stomach. The Japanese horsemen smoked their cheap, foul-smelling cigarettes and watched him. Kim wondered what had caused the change — once they had all been a happy group, working with pride to perfect their charges. Now they were ten Japanese and he was a Korean. A Korean pig, the officer had called him. They were suspicious of him, and Hirata would banish him to the mines if he dared risk Kan's anger. When he was through he rolled up his sleeping pad and took it onto the rice straw beside Flame. The little mare was stretched out flat and lifted her head as he rolled out the pad within arm reach of her.

Kim realized that moving away was a rude gesture and a final break with the Japanese. How long would the tenuous thread of Kan's authority hold and protect him?

CHAPTER VI

THE NEXT MORNING when Kim led Flame past the compound, he saw the American in the monkey cage. The cage, a cocoon of woven barbed wire, was too small for its occupant to do other than stand erect or fold into a tight knot and sit on his heels. This position could be assumed by a short-legged Oriental, but was impossible for a long-limbed American and guards were instructed that prisoners not be permitted to cling to the wire and ease the weight from fatigue-throbbing legs. It was a form of Japanese punishment all Koreans recognized. Kim knew thirty-six hours would break a man; forty-eight would put him in a state of mental and physical collapse and sixty would produce a frothing insanity from which few recovered.

Covertly Kim looked at the blond giant. Stripped to the waist and barefoot, the American's face was haggard and his body hunger-gaunt and drawn, and interlacing his shoulders and back were livid welts from the riding crop. Only his eyes were strong — cold, blue and undimmed.

The sight distressed Kim and he wondered how long the man must remain in the wire enclosure. It had been twenty-four hours since the rice-loading incident, yet the blond stood erect with his bare feet spread to the limits of the base of the cage and his hands locked behind his back. He reminded Kim of the Colonel's dismounted cavalrymen standing at parade rest. He appeared immobile, impervious to all, even the swarming flies on his open welts.

Kim pretended to adjust the harness. While squatting under Flame's belly and tugging at the leather straps, he noted the position of the sentry who was patrolling a safe distance away.

Kim said, "Beel Duffee—" then, in Korean, he added "my heart is with you."

The cold blue eyes warmed, "Watch yourself, Kim Huk Moon."

Kim could risk no more and taking Flame by the lead strap he moved on toward the loading platform and the stacks of bagged rice. The boy learned much in the following days. He saw the pitiful amount of rice given the prisoners for food and learned that once a week they were served a thin soya bean soup that was little better than hot water. Though the prisoners handled tons of rice a day, the guards were so strict none was able to secrete even a handful in his rugged clothing. Those who were caught were given twenty-four hours in the monkey cage.

Bill Duffy was the bellwether, the standard bearer for the others and he came from the cage unbowed, but his ribs protruded through his skin in ugly ridges and blue-black circles rimmed his eyes.

Kim worried and planned a way to get rice to his friend before the man died of starvation. Lying on the straw near Flame, he thought of scheme after scheme, only to discard them as holes of weakness appeared. One night, as a streak of lightning from a dark cloud, it came to him. The next day he bought a bamboo walking staff much like Hirata's and the groom was pleased to think the boy was aping him. That night Kim carved a tight-fitting cap to the handle joint. With the cap removed, the bamboo was hollow to the next joint and would hold three handfuls of rice. With a second staff of like size, he carved a similar cap and hid it in the straw. Then he began to fret over the language barrier between Duffy and himself.

The next day at the loading platform Kim developed a limp and leaned heavily on his staff. When the sentries were otherwise occupied, he caught the American's eye and motioned for him to begin to limp also. Duffy could not understand the pantomime, shook his head and went on with the loading of sacks. En route to Inchon Kim removed the cap of his staff and pushed the open end through the loose weave of the rice straw bags. When the bamboo came out it was filled to the first joint and, with the cap in place, no one would suspect it contained three handfuls of rice.

During the following days Kim attempted to convey to Duffy that he wanted him to become lame so there would be an excuse to lean on a staff. The American knew the boy was attempting to convey a message and his face clouded with anger for not being able to grasp its import.

One day when there was a great hullabaloo over a sack of rice that was dropped and burst open, Kim removed the cap and revealed the rice in the handle. Instantly the American's face lighted with understanding and it was not many minutes before he tumbled from the platform and set up a terrific wailing. It was so genuine that even the guards were impressed. When Duffy attempted to stand, his right ankle was like rubber and he yowled even louder.

Kim said to the Japanese NCO in charge. "Honorable Sergeant, Sir, you have the big heart of a brave fighting soldier. Allow me to give the big nose my bamboo stick so he may walk."

The sergeant considered. He blew his nose and scratched under his arm.

"It will take four men to carry such a big one back to the wire enclosure and we will be late with the loading, which will make the Honorable Lieutenant yell like he did the other day."

The sergeant said, "Give him the stick."

Kim held out the bamboo to Duffy. In a loud voice he shouted, "Here you are, clumsy big nose. Use my stick. I should beat you with it for delaying us."

Duffy took the stick and got to his feet by leaning heavily on it. The corners of his mouth jerked and his eyes were warm and slightly moist when he looked at Kim.

"I love you, Buster," he mumbled.

The next day Kim carried the staff he had buried in the straw and on the road to Inchon filled the handle with rice. The following morning he and Duffy effected an exchange. Each day this was done and Duffy, in turn, gave the rice to fellow prisoners who were suffering the worst for malnutrition. The extra rice, small as the amount was, would save the lives of several borderline starvation cases. To protect Kim and assure the Japanese would not take away his bamboo staff, Duffy beat his ankle nightly to keep it puffed and discolored.

One morning while Duffy sat on a bag of rice during the mid-morning rest period, he slipped off the cap and shoved the open bamboo through the rice straw sacking. At the noontime lock-up he emptied the rice under his sleeping pad. In the afternoon he again filled the handle and in this fashion was able to double the amount of stolen rice. At first Kim was puzzled when Duffy failed to exchange walking sticks, but he soon realized the American was doing his own stealing.

Before long another prisoner came down lame and was forced to implement his walking with a bamboo stick. Kim hugged himself with delight when he saw several more taken lame and leaning on crutches of bamboo. He hoped they would not overdo it and make the Japanese suspicious, but Duffy was aware of this danger also and would allow no more than one in fifteen to go lame.

It was two months before Kim could prevail upon Hirata to ask the Japanese officer to allow him to return to the race track to gather up horseshoes, nails and other supplies for the animals. Flame's shoes were paper thin and her hoofs were peeling — if new shoes were not soon available, her feet would be permanently maimed. Although the supplies were badly needed, Kim was more concerned over the welfare of his mother and Chung Soon and news of his father. No word had passed between them since his departure. Kim slept fitfully and was in the saddle before daylight. Flame was happy, being relieved of the hated task of hauling the rice cart, and the two of them rollicked along in a better mood than either had known since Kan and the Colonel left Korea.

Kim found the track overgrown with weeds and that vandals had broken into the stable and house. Everything of value had been stolen, but the thieves had left horseshoes and nails.

He put Flame in the charge of an old man whom he trusted while he took a trolley into the city to withdraw some money. At the bank he received the distressing news that a government ruling had been passed whereby funds were automatically invested in war bonds. Kim did not understand such procedure and the Japanese teller grew angry and shouted at him. Instead of having five hundred fifty-three yen, he had five war bonds worth a hundred yen each and fifty-three yen he could withdraw if he wished. This he did. He considered the bonds worthless and his money in the bank had been the anchor to the hope that someday, some way, he could buy Flame. His disappointment was so great he had to fight back the tears.

Buying food and small presents, he went to the village. It was little changed save that the people looked more workworn and hungry. The old woman still sat with her back to the mud wall of her hutch and when her staring, lusterless eyes stared directly at him and there was no outcry, he realized she was blind.

He went to her. "I am Kim Hut Moon," he told her and untied his bundle and placed in her hands a small packet of tea. "I would be honored if you would accept this."

At the five street intersection his heart jumped when the police sergeant waved him over.

"What are you doing here?"

Kim handed over the paper signed by the officer at the rice collecting point. "I am to pick up horse supplies at the race track and return to the farms."

The policeman scowled as he read; he returned the paper. "What have you in the package?"

"Food for my sick mother and a present for my sister."

The officer took the package, tore off the bindings and ripped away the paper cover. An inner package burst and some of the tea spilled at his feet. More of it spilled when he thrust it roughly back into Kim's hands.

"Don't let me see you around here beyond the stated time in your pass from the army lieutenant. I have a monkey cage waiting for you."

Fighting to control his anger, Kim hurried down the street. When out of the policeman's sight, he reshaped the package so that it looked more like a present.

Chung Soon saw him and came flying to meet him. Her face told him what he feared as she clung to him for a long moment. In silence they walked into the house where Mother Kim sat on a sleeping pad before the stove. She made him think of the poor blind woman he had just seen.

After a time he left them and made his way to the shrine in the mulberry orchard where he wrote a prayer and placed it on the wheel. It was easier now to understand why his father had hated the Japanese, and he realized that if it were not for Kan and Takeo and the Colonel, he would hate the invaders of his country as much as his father had. After paying the Buddhist monk, he walked slowly back to the village. In the market place he bought a heavy cover because Chung Soon had told him the mother was sleeping cold at night. His resentment flared anew when he counted the remaining yen. There were only twelve left and he wanted to grind the war bonds into the dirt.

Late that night Kim returned to the track and slept in the stall with Flame. Before daylight he led the little mare to a smithy they both knew and, with borrowed tools, pared and trimmed her feet and fitted on new shoes. It was apparent that Flame thought this meant a return to the life she loved. For the sake of old times, he took her on a gallop around the grass grown course. She struck her vain, arch-necked gait and it was not difficult for the boy to imagine the crowd once again was cheering them. Much of the fire left her when he put a pack behind the saddle and turned her southward.

Tragedy struck the day following Kim's return to the rice-collecting point. One of the prisoners dropped his bamboo staff — the cap flew off and rice spilled onto the ground. Amidst loud yelling, beatings and swearing, all walking sticks were collected; and were found to contain stolen rice. The sergeant of the guard remembered Kim presenting the bamboo to Duffy. Without asking for a confession or allowing a denial, he descended on the boy with maniacal fury and beat him into an unconscious state.

The excitement was too much for high-strung Flame, and matching the savagery about her, she went berserk and kicked her way free of the hated cart and harness.

When Kim regained his senses he was in a barbed wire cage. It was a long time before his eyes would focus and he could make out Duffy in the cage next to him. It was still longer before he could move and when he did it brought such pain he groaned.

Duffy, his huge body a cross section of welts, heard the boy. Through puffed lips and over a cotton-dry tongue, his voice was a growl.

"I'm sorry I got you into this, Buster, but our day will come. Live! Live for it! The day we win this war will be the Day of Judgment."

Forty-eight hours later Kim was taken from the cage and thrown into the stall with Flame as a concession to the animal. Since the day she had kicked her way free of the cart, she would allow the other handlers to water and feed her, but at the mere suggestion of placing her in harness she went into a fury that scattered Mirata and the others like dry leaves in a wind. She was an outlaw and Hirata came to know sleepless nights as he thought of meeting again with Kan.

Kim never did remember the days or how many there were before he awakened one morning to find Chung Soon bathing him. She had left Mother Kim in the house of Schoolmaster Yu and made the journey to deliver a letter from Takeo. The boy's first regard was for Flame and he leaned weakly against the horse as his hand ran over her body. She was thin and it was not until she was fed and watered that he took the letter into the light. A blinding pain darting across his eyes made standing erect difficult.

Carefully folded in the heavy envelope were five one hundred yen notes. Kim looked about quickly as he pocketed the bills. Good old Takeo. He would not forget that money was needed for feed and supplies. He smiled at Chung Soon — money worries were over now and they could buy winter wood and food. He began to read. The first words brought a tremor to his hands and his face grew pinched and old. Turning toward the stall he went to the horse and pressed his throbbing head into her mane.

"Kan was killed in battle."

He sat in the straw and Chung Soon settled beside him with her arm about his shoulders. His breathing was so heavy she turned her head that she might not embarrass him to see him crying.

"We must not tell Hirata. It is all that keeps Flame and me together."

It was several weeks before Kim was able to work, and even then his headaches persisted and there were times when the pain was such as to blind him. It took even longer to cajole Flame into accepting harness again.

The boy coaxed and used every persuasion with the little mare because Hirata had told him, on direct orders from the army lieutenant, that if she did not work she would not eat. Patience and love accomplished the task and one day Flame accepted the harness, and they were assigned to hauling the night soil cart through the camp while prisoners emptied latrine buckets into it. It was a demeaning job and Kim was aware it was a studied insult because Hirata had lost face in being unable to handle the horse and the others had laughed at his failure. The groom's hatred for the boy and Flame became a heavy thing. He drew up a letter of false accusations and mailed it to Kan.

There was one redeeming feature to the foul job as it brought Kim in contact with Duffy again. The big blond and the others caught carrying rice-concealing bamboo staffs had been put on half rations and given the most degrading jobs. Under heavy guard Duffy and four others had been assigned to the night soil cart. The boy was distressed at the sight of his friend. His cheeks were sunken and the eyes were like the blue sky shining through the holes of a skull. Kim knew the man would not live if more food wasn't put into his stomach sack.

One evening Kim slipped away and made his way into Anyang. He searched through the market with care to find food in tins. After some thought, he decided on canned tangerines; the fruit would prevent beriberi and the sugar syrup would give quick strength. He also bought canned fish. Upon his return to camp he placed the tins in a latrine bucket and covered them over with the slop from another. He went to sleep happy in the knowledge his friend would fill the corners of his gnawing stomach before another night passed.

He had been asleep only a short time when a searing pain over his left eye brought him awake with a scream. Moaning softly, he rocked back and forth until the pain subsided.

The next morning Kim led Flame and the horrendous-smelling cart into the wire enclosure. Duffy and his fellow prisoners were waiting for them at the gate. The soldier guards did not follow them on their rounds inside the wire, but lighted cigarettes and waited at the gate. Once out of sight, Kim poured off the refuse in the bucket with the tins of food.

Duffy knew his life was in those tins. He patted the boy's shoulder. "As I said before, Buster, I love you."

Kim soon discovered there were other advantages to the job. For the most part, they were through by mid-afternoon and the roads about the prison encampment were easier on Flame's feet than the one to Inchon. When the rice crop was harvested and hauled to the harbor town, the paddies had to be prepared for a second crop. The sight of the other horses hauling ploughs through the knee-deep muck of the fields made Kim realize Hirata's revenge was really a blessing.

To the west of the enclosure Kim discovered a broad-backed paddy dike. It was more than a half mile in length and was free of rocks and potholes. Gaining reluctant permission from Hirata, the boy began taking his charge for a gallop in the cool of the evenings. Kim was becoming increasingly concerned over the knotty muscles that cart hauling was developing in Flame and he hoped the nightly exercise would bring back her running legs.

Life settled into an uneasy pattern. Twice a week food was transferred to Duffy and the American was showing the effects of his supplemented food allowance. Twice Chung Soon made her way south for night visits. Mother Kim was improved with the extra food and warmth from the wood purchased with Takeo's money. Nam Soon was living with them now that her husband had been drafted into a Korean Labor Battalion and shipped overseas. She had a baby boy now five months old and a second child was on its way.

Chung Soon's third visit brought a letter from Takeo which struck alarm in Kim's heart. The old trainer wrote that Kan's family had turned over Hirata's damning letter to him for answering. The old man counseled peace; they must not allow disagreements to work to the harm of the horses. They were horsemen and the animals were their first concern and responsibility. Anger should not disrupt them; they owed it to the memory of his Excellency the Colonel and to the man they all had loved — Kan, the number one.

Despite the kind words, Kim knew Hirata would banish him if he ever learned Kan was dead. Takeo's letter to the groom must be at the post office near the track. Chung Soon must go to the post office and ask for mail held there for all the Japanese, and burn the letters.

As she prepared to leave, she asked Kim to walk with her for a short distance. When they were alone on the road, she told him that Schoolmaster Yu had told her the war was going badly for the Japanese; that she acted as messenger for him and meetings were being held and plans laid for a new government once the Nipponese were defeated. Kim was startled by the news. He had never dreamed the Japanese would be defeated. What would that mean to Flame, he wondered? No matter what happened, peace or war, they must never be separated. He watched Chung Soon down the road until she was out of sight.

Though his head pained severely, he saddled Frame and they went for a gallop on the dike. That night he suffered a searing, tearing pain over his left eye. He had experienced many such attacks, but this was much the worst. He was wet and trembling when it finally passed.

In the morning, for the first time, he noticed he was nearly blind in his left eye. When he held his hand over his right eye, all he could see were shadows.

As slowly as a tule fog slipping away from low ground, changes occurred in the Japanese personnel of the prison encampment. Those who had been cruel and savage walked with fear in their eyes and no longer went into the enclosure alone. The ration of rice for the prisoners was increased and doctors made a show of concern over the health and welfare of their charges. Less and less work was required of the Americans in the fields and a blanket of tense waiting covered the land. No longer were heard the shouting and cursing of guards and the sodden blows of clubs on bowed backs. No one had been thrown into the wire cages for many weeks.

One evening Hirata came into the room where Flame and Kim lived. He smiled and offered the boy a cigarette.

Kim shook his head, "I do not smoke."

Hirata squatted on his heels and nodded pleasantly as though the obvious rudeness of the refusal went unnoticed. He sucked on his cigarette, he spit on the straw and scratched at his belly. Words came with difficulty.

"I think you should be number one again."

Kim lowered his left eyelid so the fuzziness from that eye would not interfere with seeing his enemy.

"Why?" he asked.

"You know, Worthy Kim, I never wanted to take your place, but that miserable Army officer made me. He would have killed me if I'd refused."

"Do you remember the day the rice was found in the walking sticks?"

Hirata nodded and the forced smile left his lips.

"Do you remember how you joined the guards in beating us? When the war is over and the Americans are turned free, I would not like to be you. I tremble to think of what they will do to you." Kim untied Flame's lead strap and took the horse for a walk along the dike.

It all happened overnight. The next morning Hirata was gone. So was the savage sergeant of the guard as well as the lieutenant. All who remained were those Japanese who had done their duty fairly and without cruelty. The rest had taken to the hills.

The gate of the enclosure was open and the Americans were milling around and shouting and laughing. Duffy saw Kim lead Flame from the hutch, and came running. He threw his arms about the boy and swung him in great circles. There were tears in his blue eyes and unashamedly he held Kim close and hugged him.

"I love you, Buster!" Duffy shouted and waved his long arms to the surrounding, shouting prisoners. Duffy quieted them.

"If it wasn't for this kid, a lot of us wouldn't have made it. Before we head for Inchon we've gotta see what we can do for him. Get that Jap translator over here."

The translator, an anemic little man wearing heavy glasses, was dragged from the administration building into the center of the circle.

Duffy said, "You're all right, Mr. Moto. We're not going to hurt you." The Japanese wet his lips and smiled briefly. "Tell our friend here, Kim Huk Moon, that we are proud to be his friend. Tell him we want to do something for him. Ask him what he wants most of all in this whole, wide, beautiful world."

Kim listened carefully to the interpreter. He asked that the last be repeated.

"The big nose says—"

Kim glared. "You will not call him that! It is not his fault his nose is like a wall between his eyes. He is my friend and you will call him, the Honorable American."

The Japanese gulped. He said slowly, "The Most Honorable American is your friend. He wants to know what you wish most of all in this life."

Kim looked at Duffy and then he looked at Flame. He began to tremble as he had at the track railing ten years before.

"Tell my worthy American friend I would rather own this horse than live until tomorrow."

Kim's wish was made known. Duffy nodded as though he had guessed as much. Telling the other Americans they should be ready to leave for Inchon in an hour, he led Kim and the interpreter to the administration building. When suitable heavy paper was found that pleased him and the Japanese had his writing brush poised, Duffy began to dictate: "To those whom it may concern: In acknowledgment of the loyalty and courage of one, Kim Huk Moon —"

CHAPTER VII

KIM AND FLAME RETURNED to Seoul. They skylarked all the way and the boy read and reread the letter given him by Duffy. He even read it to the horse and she appeared to understand it was something important and would go into her rocking horse gait. It was a happy day for both.

At the track they found disrepair and weeds. Vandals had torn away doors and all burnable materials and the stables looked hollow-eyed and gaunt. Kim found an old beggar, Lee Bok Won, living in one of the stalls.

He said to him, "Old man, you know this horse and you know me. At night you sleep in her stall and guard her. I have nothing but Japanese money and it is worthless, but I will see that your rice bowl is filled each day. When racing starts again I will have money and you will have money."

They rubbed Flame down and put her in the same stall she had occupied before the war. Scouring the area, they found enough lumber to make a door and from the infield pulled sufficient grass to feed her. Then Kim wandered about the track in a fog of nostalgic memories. Here he had stood, a trembling little boy, peering over the rail at Flame and Kan — dear, honorable Kan who was his brother. And here he had clung to the leather reins of the lunging stallion. Here it all began with Takeo and Kan. These men he loved, yet his people hated the Japanese. He hated the sergeant who had beaten him blind and the policeman who had sent his father away to die. He despised poor, mean Hirata, but he felt about these men as he did because they were mean men, not because they were Japanese. All Japanese were not cruel and hateful any more than all Koreans were good and kind.

Tears were in his eyes as he walked the rough track and he wished he could turn time backward to the happy days when they were together. As he entered the stall, Flame turned to him and he held her head close. She sensed his mood and leaned in to him.

At home Kim found his sisters in the yard with the children. Nam Soon's youngest was learning to walk and had no memory of him, but the older boy Yon came running. For the first time Kim had no little present for the child. Mother Kim was inside the house and not far from the stove, though it was a warm day. He looked at this withered, fragile woman and thought of a hillside flower in the late fall.

After the first babble of greetings was over, Kim learned of a happy circumstance. On Schoolmaster Yu's advice, Chung Soon had spent all her Japanese money for food before the war ended and the yen became worthless. No matter what happened, there would be food for some time. This had been a worry to the boy, and more than ever he realized what a debt he owed Chung Soon.

Two clouds darkened the boy's horizon. The headaches he suffered were not so frequent nor so violent, but the sight of the left eye was completely gone. This worried him because it would affect his riding in races. He was thankful it was the left eye because he could still see the rail through his right. Riding Flame would be safe for she knew more about racing than he did, but if he was to be a number one rider, he must accept the risk of riding ill-trained horses. He told no one, not even Chung Soon, of his injury.

The other problem was Nam Soon's husband. Only one letter had been received since he had been shipped overseas in a Korean labor unit. His letter had stated he was in the 204th Naval Construction Battalion; that he was on an island and the work was heavy; that he was well, but was longing for the day when he could return to his family in the Land of Chosen.

Kim took the letter to a government building in the center of the city. In a confusion of hallways, endless queues of people and harried clerks, he finally came on a sweating, overworked fellow. The man read the letter and checked the information with a mass of papers.

He told Kim, "Your brother-in-law was with the Japanese forces on the island of Iwo Jima. There were no Korean survivors from that battle."

With a heavy heart Kim took the news to his sister. Her grief was uncontrollable. Two days later her body was found in the Han River. When Chung Soon came running to the track, Kim put his arm about her and wiped her tears and held her close.

"Little sister, we now have a family."

Kim worked long and patiently with Flame. The mare, now twelve years old, came to condition slowly. There were days when she would have that long, smooth stride that made Kim think of oil slipping from a spigot. But, for the most part, it appeared to be hard labor for her to run. The spirit and heart were still there, but the rice carts of Anyang had stolen the vibrance from her muscles. Kim knew she could not regain her old form, but blinded himself with the optimism of love.

The boy put himself through an equally rigorous program of learning to see all that must be seen in a race, with one eye. His ears and senses must tell him when a horse was slipping up on his blind side. He welcomed impromptu brushes with other horses. Such small races were good for Flame and better for himself.

The wheel of time spun slowly. A Korean government was formed and the agriculture department opened a horse farm on the island of Che Ju. Many horses previously owned by Japanese were shipped to the island to form the foundation stock. The Seoul City Race Club was formed and Chung II Bin was elected president. More and more horses returned to training at the track, but all were suffering from cart-horse muscles developed during the war. The stables were repaired and the ground cleaned until the look of the old days returned and then, one day, the dates for the first race meet were announced.

And it was time, Kim thought. If it were not for their great and dear friend, the scholarly Yu, there would be no food in the Kim house. The boy aimed his training schedule to bring Flame to peak condition, and he told her, "You're running for rice now, little one. Just give me this one race and I'll ask no more."

The first day of the race meet was a gala occasion. It was more than a festival; it was a manifestation of freedom by the freedom-loving Koreans. The people began to arrive early and before the first of the morning races, the grounds were packed. By midday when the better horses were to run, the crowd was a straining, seething mass. It was said there were nearly a hundred thousand present.

The shadows were long and the day cooler when the seven horses in the feature race walked toward the barrier. Kim had drawn number five position, which put him in the middle. There was much seesawing and jostling for advantage as the starter sent them back for a more even walk-up. Twice the horse on Kim's blind side slammed into Flame and for the first time cool, confident Flame was unsettled. Kim shouted angrily at the rider on his left. Thus diverted, he missed the starting signal and they were the last away.

Flame wanted to fling herself at the leaders and run them down, but Kim eased her into stride and tried to console her into a more rational pace. Kicking up a blizzard of clod and cutting dirt, the pack went into and around the first turn. On straightening out for the long run down the back stretch, Kim gave the signal and the little mare began her move. But something was missing. In the days gone by she would reach a fast turn of speed and flash past slower horses at a pace that was heartbreaking to them. Now it was an inch by inch gain and it was hard labor.

Kim knew she was running to her limit and there were still three ahead of them; he also knew that no horse could run all out for long. He collected her and eased her back for a breathing spell. For the distance of two hundred meters Flame ran on the heels of the three leaders who were abreast and nose-to-nose. As the threesome went into the turn, a dart of light shone between the rail and the pole horse. Kim and Flame saw it at the same time and they rushed into it. Keeping his eye on the rail, Kim shifted his weight to the left to meet the bumping he felt would come, for the rider was Choi Chang, a lusty, rough one. Choi yelled and came over on them. Kim met the weight and kept Flame off the dangerous railing. Fighting doggedly to keep on her feet, the little horse wedged and drove herself farther into danger.

Unable to see the horse on his left and the rail at the same time, Kim tried to judge the rhythm of the jostler and met each thrust with all his weight. Slowly, inexorably, Flame fought forward until she was eye to eye with her rival, but Kim knew she was through, exhausted. Her stride had shortened and was jerky, and as he looked down the long straight-away to the finish line, he knew that even her great heart could not carry her that far.

And then it happened. As Choi came over with all his weight for a final lunge that would knock Flame and Kim into the rail, his stirrup strap broke. With a scream he went down. The riderless horse swerved to the outside and further impeded the others. In an instant Kim and Flame were in the clear and ran free to the wire.

Her gait was so rough he was in a panic that she was badly-injured. He eased her to a stop as soon as he could and slipped from the saddle. Her legs were cut and bleeding and her left quarter torn and the shoe missing from the hoof, but the injuries were not serious. He led her slowly back to the winner's circle. There was no rocking horse show from Flame this day and Kim knew she would never race again. It was a long walk to the stable and neither of them heard the cheering crowd.

Through the months that followed, Kim searched for a stallion to mate with Flame. There were always shortcomings in the blood lines or conformation or disposition. He must have a horse with the blood of kings in its veins and the "look of the eagle" in its eyes. Then he remembered the stallion from Pusan.

With the money Flame earned in her last race, Kim was able to repay Schoolmaster Yu and to insure food for Chung Soon and the children for some time. The boy rode other horses with indifferent success due to his partial blindness, but was able to earn enough to take care of beggarman Won and himself, without digging into his reserves. Always, of course, was his concern and care of Flame as he waited for her month of delivery to arrive.

As the day grew nearer, Chung Soon began to chide him over the hours he spent in the stall.

"You would think," she told him, "that this is the first mare in the history of the world to have a colt. You are going to fuss her into a state of nerves, which will do her no good. Come home now and rest."

Kim went home for the evening meal, but returned to the stable to spend the night. It was three o'clock in the morning when he sent Won running for the horse doctor. As the red sun of June came over the Han, the newly foaled filly stood on trembling legs and suckled the soothing colostrum of its first meal. Kim smoothed the sweat-streaked neck of Flame and the mare leaned her head against him.

"What a fine one, Flame, and just like you except for her one red stocking. And that is good or I could never tell you apart when she grows." Kim was so happy he felt the tears starting and he kissed the blaze where it was widest between her eyes.

Three mornings later Kim was terrorized when he opened the stall door to find Flame dripping with sweat and head hanging. Won ran for the doctor and the man did what he could. He kept mumbling, "Fever, it is the fever. One can do so little with this sort of fever."

Kim did not leave the stall and Chung Soon brought him food and tried to console him. On the seventh day at dawn she came to the stall to find Kim sitting in the straw stroking Flame's head. After a time she was able to coax him from the place and they took a long walk through the mulberry orchards and along the riverbank. When they returned, Won had taken care of things and the stall was empty save for the little red filly. As with horsemen the world over, those at the Seoul track rallied to the aid of a stricken fellow.

The rider, Choi Chang Ju, who had tried so desperately to win from Flame in her last race, took charge of the grief-dumb Kim.

"I have a mare who dropped a foal three days ago. She is big and strong; she can feed two as well as one. Come with me, Worthy Rider, and we will see your new Flame winning races in no time."

Kim saw his week-old filly to its foster mother's side and then left the track. The place was wrapped in so many memories he did not have it in his heart to return. He sat in the sun with his back against the wall of the old hutch and grieved. A sad mischance brought a long-delayed letter from Japan. Takeo had been dead for months. To the boy, this broke the circle. Kan, Flame and Takeo were gone and he was alone. For ten times a thousand times he abused himself for having mated the little mare. Flame would be alive if it were not for his own greed in wanting another horse. And he came to hate the filly who looked like Flame save for the one red stocking.

The summer passed and the November race meet began. On still moments during the afternoon the shouts of the people could be heard, but Kim did not heed and Chung watched him with grave concern. Choi was taking fine care of his "twins" as he called his charges and he counseled Chung Soon not to hurry Kim in his present mood.

Kim was jerked back to reality when he saw Chung Soon on her way to work in the rice paddies. That could mean only one thing — there was no more money. He put on his riding clothes and went to the track and announced he was ready to accept mounts. He rode in three races and won all of them. There was an exhilaration of achievement and he felt better, but he did not go to the stable area where the little red filly was housed. Choi had several horses now and hired Kim to ride them, and from time to time he would report on the filly's condition, but never suggested a personal inspection.

The filly was sixteen months old before Kim saw her again. He was entering the gate by the grandstand one early morning when he froze in his tracks and the breath whistled from his throat. Flame was in the center field with other youngsters, but the boy had no eyes for any but the little red. She tired of feeding and, ranging alongside her "twin," roughed and jostled it and then broke away in a rocking horse gait. It was Flame come to life! There was a purity of motion about her that Kim had seen only in one other horse and the hatred drained from his heart and he felt mean.

In an ecstasy, the filly continued her romp to the far end of the field and was turning when three dogs broke from under the rail and rushed at her. In a moment the scene was changed as the terrified filly tried to run back to her mates, but the vicious dogs savaged her with two at her front and one leaping for her hams.

Kim was over the rail with a bound. Terror lent speed to his limbs and he ran as never before. His shouts distracted the dogs momentarily and Flame broke from the fang-ringed circle, and with a cry of fear she raced to him. The more vicious leader dog followed and was met by Kim's foot.

Trembling with fright, the filly came close to Kim and leaned her head against him. The boy slipped his arm about her neck and held her close.

"I'm sorry, Flame, I'm sorry," he whispered. After a time he led her to the old stall and put her inside. He rubbed until her fright was gone and then stood away from her. "It's about time you learn to be a running horse." When he left the stall he was a little surprised that Kan and Takeo were not waiting for him.

The filly came to hand quickly, eagerly. She had more intelligence than Kim had known in a horse and there was a searching curiosity about her that was nearly human. There was an eagerness to learn that made training little more than showing her once. Before their reunion was three months old, Kim was forced to admit that the filly had qualities never shown by her mother. And then a strange thing occurred. It was something Kim was unable to explain to himself as he realized there had been but one Flame. Now he knew what the Buddhist monk meant when he spoke of reincarnation. He went to the temple and placed a prayer of thanks on the wheel.

Each day Kim brought Nam Soon's son Yon to the track and the boy showed a keen interest in horses. Because of his light weight, he was the first to ride Flame in her early training with Kim on the lead rope. Then one day Kim mounted her and onto the track they went and he gulped when she broke into her rocking horse gait. Day after day, week after week, the filly went to school and her talents and speed increased. In racing brushes with other horses she sped away from them and was as delighted with herself as was her rider. The summer race meet in July was announced and Kim pointed her training to the big day.

One late afternoon, as he was putting Flame away for the night, Choi came running.

"War has started!" he shouted.

"War?" Kim answered, thinking of the day Kan had told him of another war. "War with the Japanese again?"

"No, no! The communists from the North country are fighting us."

Kim frowned and ran his hand along Flame's neck: "They are Korean people."

"Yes, yes, but they are communist Koreans."

"What does that mean, friend Choi?"

"If they win, it means we will live as we lived under the Japanese. It means they will take away our horses. Under them no man may even own the air he breathes. I am sending my horses south with my old father. I will join the army to fight these invaders."

Kim nodded and remembered the Chinese tattooed man. From then on he thought of communists as being like that man.

"I will take my ancient mother south to Pusan and then I will join you."

Mother Kim refused to leave the old mud hutch she had lived in so many years. Kim pleaded with her and made her listen, to the crash of heavy guns moving nearer and nearer. The sight of her neighbors packing and fleeing, prevailed at last and a hurried collection of belongings began. Improvising a harness, Flame was put to an abandoned night-soil cart. Into this Kim packed the sleeping mats, cooking jars and food. On top went his mother and the children. With Chung beside him he took the lead strap and they joined the endless queue of frightened people. The filly accepted the strange assignment without fuss or complaint.

At the five-street intersection, Kim and Chung stopped when they heard the wailing cry of the old woman. Kim went to her and taking her in his arms, placed her in the cart alongside his mother. He was surprised at the lightness of her — she weighed no more than a half-filled rice bag.

Such slow progress was made that it was past midnight before they were near the ferry site. Obviously there would be no crossing at this point with frantic thousands waiting ahead of them, and it was impossible to continue along the river and cross at the Yongdongpo Bridge. Turning inland, Kim led his party through a mulberry orchard and across a rice paddy. It was rough going for those in the cart, but the old women hung on grimly. When clear of the pack of humanity, Kim again turned. This time in the direction of his home village. Above the village of Chusong-Jong he made his way to the river-bank.

"We must swim the river," he whispered to Chung Soon.

Unhitching Flame from the cart, Kim took her to the water's edge. She looked out over the dark coil of water and appeared to know what they were to do — the air came whistling from her nostrils in anticipation.

Cautioning the old women to remain in the cart with the children, Kim turned to Chung Soon.

"Hang onto Flame's tail. She will swim you across."

Kim removed the headstall and with his hand on the filly's mane moved into the water beside her. The river was shallow from summer drought and they were quite some distance from the bank before Flame let out a snort and began to swim. Kim trailed beside her with his fingers woven in her mane.

"Are you all right?" he called to Chung Soon.

"Yes, yes."

Kim guessed Flame swam three hundred meters before her feet came to bottom again. Another period of wading and they stood on the southern bank. In the darkness they searched out a flat, smooth campsite.

"You wait here. I will send Flame back with the children. You meet her and send her back."

"Is that safe? Sending her alone?"

"She has many crossing to make and she can't do it with me hanging to her side."

Kim pointed Flame into the river again and was towed to the northern bank. He lifted Yon from the cart and onto her back.

"Hold on tight and Flame will take you to Chung Soon," he directed.

Without order the filly headed into the river while Kim stood to his knees in water and followed their progress by the sound of her swimming. He shivered; the water was colder than he had expected. He was becoming anxious with the waiting when he heard Flame swimming, and soon she stood beside him. He held her head close to his wet body and waited until her breathing was normal before lifting little Nam Soon onto her back. The child was near to hysteria and refused to go alone. So once again Flame had to tow Kim and carry Nam Soon.

Mother Kim, too, was terrified by the thought of crossing the river with the horse. Patiently Kim explained that it had to be done, that it was safe and that the little horse was a strong swimmer, but her terror refused to wash away with his assurances. Finally he lifted her from the cart and carried her to the water's edge. Interlocking his fingers in Flame's tail, he spoke to the filly and she moved forward.

It was desperately hard work towing the two, and the crossing was slow. When the little horse touched the far shore she stood with head hanging and flanks heaving. Kim left her and carried his mother ashore. She was moaning from the shock of the experience and the chill of the water. Chung Soon held her close in an effort to warm her old bones, but to no avail.

The filly had recovered somewhat when Kim returned and she turned back into the water again. On the northern shore Kim found the cart empty, the old woman gone. Running along the bank and calling loudly, he searched and searched without success. Streaks of dawn were showing in the east when he was forced to admit that his charge was not to be found. Making a bundle of rice, sleeping pads and clothing, he secured them to Flame's back and crossed the Han for the last time. It was well, for the filly was trembling from exhaustion.

The succeeding days and nights brought a hunted life to Kim and his family. With Mother Kim and little Nam Soon riding, they moved southward along the gutted roads. No matter how fast they traveled, it seemed as though the sound of enemy guns remained at the same distance behind. They were heartened when they met many Americans moving northward. The Americans would soon drive out the invaders, Kim told his family as he scanned the faces, praying that he might see Duffy.

They buried Mother Kim on a hillside overlooking the Naktong River, but there was not the time, until two days later, for Kim to seek out a temple to pray for the tired old lady. She had never recovered from the night river crossing.

Pusan was chaotic and wild with rumors and the harbor filled with ships bringing supplies and men to fight against the invaders. This heartening sight did not still the panic brought by the news that American troops had been defeated and were also being driven southward.

Kim searched out his friend Lee Eyi Ja, who owned Flame's sire, and all were given food and shelter. The little sorrel was thin and gaunt and her coat had lost its sheen. Kim worked long over her before he fell onto his sleeping pad. For the first time in two weeks, they slept the night through and there was grain for the filly.

Two days of rest and Kim went into the city to join the Korean Army. They soon discovered his blind eye and he was refused armed service, but was put to work on the docks unloading American ships. In marshaling every man and animal to the job of repelling the invaders, Flame and her sire came to hauling cartloads of military supplies from the harbor to the huge dumps on the skirt of the city. And still the communist Koreans moved closer and closer to Pusan.

Kim asked Lee, "What do we do if the enemy break through and enter Pusan like they did Seoul?"

"We are in a trap. There is no place we can go from here."

One day there was a flurry of excitement as a ship was warped into the dock. Work was suspended and Kim and Lee waited in a long line of horses and carts. A Korean Army band paraded and school children with flowers in hand marched onto the dock singing. A large, black automobile moved onto the wharf and several men stepped out. Lee told Kim, "That is the mayor of Pusan with the flowers in his hand. His name is Kim Chu Han — the Honorable Kim is going to make a speech to that white-haired big nose, the one with the silver star on his shirt collar."

Kim watched the American general and thought of Duffy. He said to Lee, "He has the look of an eagle about him."

Then they listened to the words of Kim Chu Han:

"Thank you, General Craig, for bringing your Marines to fight for our country. The panic will leave my people now."

"Who are Marines?" Kim whispered.

"They are the number ones, it is they who beat the Japanese."

It was not long before Kim learned the Marines were fighting in the hills not far from his mother's grave and had thrown the invaders back into the Naktong River — and Pusan was saved. But the war went on. The work was hard and the hours long and there was never enough rice, though Chung Soon worked in the fields. At night Kim tried to forget his empty stomach by dreaming of the races Flame would run when the war was over. The next day would be the same with long hours of hard work and a small bowl of rice.

When the Marines drove the communist Koreans from Seoul, Kim prepared to return north, but Lee prevailed upon him to remain in Pusan until after the winter season. It was reported that the capital was destroyed and the food was even more scarce there than in Pusan. It was well that Kim listened to his friend, for the enemy regained Seoul in their winter offensive and further destruction was inflicted on the city.

It was a year before the boy put Flame to a cart and headed northward. Each mile brought them across scenes of destruction and the answer to the rice shortage lay before them in the crushed paddy dikes and barren fields. The Yongdongpo Bridge had been destroyed, but rebuilt so as to support single lines of traffic, and everywhere buildings were down and the red tile of their roofs lay in the streets. It was a sad return along the banks of the Han to see so many landmarks in the ruin of nibble.

Kim was torn with the pain of it. "What is there left?" he asked the little red horse plodding at his side.

In their village they found most of the buildings showing the destructive marks of war. Their home was without a roof or a north wall. Hard work put it into condition for shelter and Kim went looking for work. There was nothing at the race track as the grounds were being used by small airplanes and helicopters of the American Army. As in the other war, the race horses had become cart horses with a few still housed in their old stalls.

Yon was old enough to take care of his sister during the day, so Chung Soon went to work in the rice fields. Kim took a job earring rice from the fields to the government warehouse at the old Cavalry Barracks. Daily the hwan purchased less. Though Kim and Chung Soon labored every daylight hour, they knew light bowls of rice at night. Again Kim was forced to resort to his bamboo walking stick thievery to insure Nam Soon and Yon food enough for life. There was little grain for the filly, and the children spent the days in the hills plucking grass for her.

Choi returned to the track one day. He had lost an arm in the fighting around Wonju and was coughing badly. He had also lost his family and horses to the war. When he left to join the army he had turned the stock over to his father to take to Pusan, but that was the last he had heard or seen of them. His spirits were good, however, and he made Kim laugh with his tales of fighting. Choi was proud that his battalion had been attached to the American Army 2d Division. When he had been wounded, it was an American doctor who lopped off his left arm just below the elbow. They had given him a paper which would take him into any American military hospital and he had been promised an artificial arm when the stump was healed. It was evident Choi thought himself a lucky fellow, though he did worry a great deal about his family and was doing what he could to find trace of them.

Because he was a disabled veteran, he got a ration of rice from the government, but his spirit would not let him sit in the sun and be lazy. He joined Kim and Flame and did what he could with one arm. One night he slipped through the fence and stole a sack of barley. For some time after they all ate well on barley soup while Flame had her first grain in weeks, and her spirit returned overnight.

One afternoon little Yon came screaming along the road. The boy was babbling hysterically. At Kim's urging. Flame sped the cart over the rough roads at a reckless pace to the village. They found the house crowded with the curious and the doctor working over Chung Soon while she lay on a sleeping pad. Her lips were pulled away from her teeth in a wolfish snarl and her cries filled the room. Kim learned what had happened — while working in the fields someone had stepped on a land mine. Four people had been killed and several hurt. Chung Soon had lost her left leg. The doctor already had removed the mangled limb.

Kim motioned his neighbors from the house and asked the doctor, "What can be done?"

"There is nothing more I can do. Hospital beds are all for the soldiers. I cannot even get the drugs I need."

Choi said, "Write down what you should have. I will get it."

Kim went to his sister and, sitting beside her, lifted her head onto his lap. His gentle hand stroked the cold, damp forehead. She opened her eyes and recognized him.

"Rest, little sister, rest."

When she was asleep he went into the yard. He was shocked to see Choi white-faced and grim, beating the stump of his arm with a stick.

"Have you gone crazy?" Kim cried.

Choi rose; he swayed dizzily. "I will go to the University Hospital now. When they see my stump they will admit me for treatment. Come to visit me tomorrow. I will have the drugs for little Chung Soon."

The next day it took nearly two hours for Kim to gain admittance to the hospital. The surly American sentry made him remember the Japanese soldier at the cavalry barracks gate many years before. Choi had the promised drugs and the sad news that he would be confined for several days because of the inflammation in his arm — he had beaten it too hard. As Kim left the hospital grounds he saw several Korean soldiers taking their first steps with artificial limbs.

Two days later Choi showed up with an American doctor. Choi babbled happily that this was the man who had taken off his arm after the Battle of Wonju; he was now at the University Hospital and they had met by accident in the hallway but the doctor had remembered him.

After that it was easier. The doctor came to call nearly every day and brought food as well as medicine. One day he arrived with a jeep load of food and the news that he was leaving Korea. It was a sad parting and their hearts were filled, but all was not sorrow for Chung Soon was able to walk to the door on the crutches he had brought her.

After the doctor drove away, Kim and Choi sat against the wall smoking American cigarettes. Kim said, "I must get one of those legs for Chung Soon. You know, the kind I see the soldiers wearing at the hospital."

Choi turned a long face to Kim. "I have asked. They are very expensive unless you are a soldier. For Chung Soon it would cost much money, I cannot bring myself to steal one from an honorable soldier who has given a leg to our Land of Chosen. Besides, each one is made to fit."

"You have done enough, good friend. It is up to me to get a leg for Chung Soon. I cannot let her hobble about on those crutches. She has spent her life taking care of me. It is my turn now. I will get her a leg. Once I wanted to own Flame more than I wanted my next breath. I did own Flame; I own Flame's image. And now I want a leg for Chung — I will get such a leg."

The weeks slipped by and the coolness of late October was in the air. Kim and Choi finished their hauling early one day and hurried to the track. They saddled Flame and Kim took her for a gallop on the long unused track. The filly responded and skylarked with the joy of running free again. When American airmen gathered at the rail to watch, she began her vain, rocking horse gait and they applauded.

Choi held her while Kim rubbed her down and the two talked about the days to come when the war would be over and there would be racing again. They put the filly in the stall with a feed of hoarded grain and were about to leave when three Americans drove up in a jeep. Proud of knowing their language, Choi spoke to them. After many words back and forth, Choi said to Kim, "They are looking for a horse. They want to buy a horse to carry ammunition. They are Marines; you know, the number ones."

Kim looked at the officer and thought of Duffy — the same good, clear eyes. He turned sick inside and wanted to run away; he wanted to rush into Flamed stall and slam the door shut that they might not see her.

Without speaking or moving, he watched Choi and the American move along the stalls and peer inside. Kim closed his eyes and waited when the officer unlatched the door and stepped into the stall with Flame. He didn't open them until Choi called, "He wants to buy Flame!"

Kim gritted his teeth. "Tell him to go away."

Choi whistled "He will pay in American green money. He will pay two hundred and fifty dollars."

Kim's throat was stiff, parched. "Will that buy a leg for Chung?"

Choi saw his friend's face. He whispered, "Yes, my brother, it will buy a leg."

"Tell him to leave the stall." When they were outside Kim entered and closed the door. Flame turned to him and leaned her head against him. He held her close. "I'm sorry, Flame, I'm sorry. Anyunghee keh sipseeyah."

Kim helped load the little sorrel into the trailer and watched them out of sight. Without looking at Choi he went into the stall and closed the door. The strength left his legs and he slumped in the corner. For the first time since Kim Huk Moon was eight, he cried.

PART TWO

CHAPTER I

IT WAS NEITHER by accident nor frivolous whim that Flame came to join the Marine Corps. A young Marine officer recognized the necessity of having a horse to carry ammunition for his recoilless rifles. At a cost of $250 to himself he filled this need (and a junior officer, with family, is intimate with the contents of his purse). It was no accident, either, that Flame should become a legend in a corps of men which breeds legends. The whole pattern of her life had been based on loyalty and steadfastness.

Explanations as to the military situation at this time must be borne to understand why Lt. Eric Pedersen drove to the Seoul race track on that October day to purchase a horse.

Fighting in the vicinity of the truce-talk village of Panmunjom (called Yak Yak Town by the Marines) placed restrictions on United Nations troops in the sector. When Panmunjom was selected as a site for the meeting place, the negotiators drew a circle on a map. This circle was 2,000 meters in diameter with Panmunjom at the hub. Both sides agreed not to fire into, over or through this circle. Inasmuch as Panmunjom was 5,000 meters forward of the United Nations Main Line of Resistance (MLR), it was necessary to establish a neutral corridor through which United Nations personnel could move to and from meetings. This strip, 200 meters wide, was to be held inviolate, as was the circle.

Other strictures were placed on the United Nations troops. A larger circle with a two-mile radius was established and aircraft were not allowed to fly over this territory. Other lines were drawn: A corps NO FIRE LINE, a NO VOICE BROADCAST LINE, a NO AIRCRAFT WEST OF THIS LINE and a NO LEAFLET DROPPING LINE. These lines of prohibition were drawn by the United Nations command as insurance no overt act would be committed to give the enemy cause for anger.

A thousand meters east of the Panmunjom circle was Combat Outpost No. 2. It was manned by nearly 300 Marines. Besides the usual sector weapons, it mustered mortars, both 60 mm. and Si's, three tanks and two Quad 50's. It was a stronghold, a fortress and its proximity to Panmunjom was a festering thorn to the CCF (Communist Chinese Forces) and a contradiction to their propaganda that they controlled the entire area about Panmunjom; that the Americans were going to their site to plead a truce.

They wanted to remove this barb, but were unwilling to pay the price of five thousand casualties. With considerable military cunning they devised a plan whereby they could gain COP 2 and other outposts along the line without paying an exorbitant cost.

COP 2 was only one segment of a battalion sector. There was the Main Line and other outposts, and all were interdependent. The loss of one would weaken the rest, and in certain cases, make the line untenable.

The battalion sector which anchored its left flank on COP 2 had as a right flank bastion the busy, noisy outpost called Bunker. Five hundred yards to the left (west) of Bunker was vulnerable Hedy, with cool and calm Ingrid yet another five hundred meters to the west. The Chinese command had a desire for Hedy too, because much of the main line would have to be abandoned in that sector if it were to come under their control.

Due to the topography, however, Ingrid could halt or hinder any large attack on Hedy because the CCF must make their approach through an area known as Hedy's Crotch. The Marines on Ingrid could take enemy troops moving into the crotch under heavy, flanking fire. Aware of this, the Chinese resorted to trickery to gain Hedy as they were doing in the case of COP 2.

Twelve hundred meters farther left lay compact, confident Outpost Kate — named by a young Marine from Ohio who was true to his schoolgirl sweetheart, even to the point of not being influenced by pin-up pictures in his bunker. And still another 1,000 meters west was high-breasted Marilyn. Nearly impervious to attack, Marilyn could support outpost Kate to her right and COP 2, 2,000 meters to the west.

Facing these positions from more northern and usually higher ground, lay the positions of the enemy Chinese. Frowning down on Bunker and Hedy and Ingrid were the mighty Taedok Song and bull-shouldered Yoke. Poised and ever dangerous to Marilyn and Kate were the Claw, Three Fingers and the Boot. Hill 90, at the foot of Marilyn and just cut of reach of Three Fingers, was the scene of nightly fighting. Neither side wanted title to this bit of real estate, yet neither could afford to allow the other occupancy.

Enemy strong points facing on COP 2 were more phlegmatic in name, yet contained the usual enemy vitriol — Hills 82, 84 and 138. The Marines came up with two graphic names in this sector, Toothache and Molar. Toothache was so called because it was in that no-shoot area between COP 2 and the holy circle and was a constant pain to the Marines. Molar was named for the simple reason that on the map it looked like an extracted molar.

The distance between friendly and enemy positions was dictated by the distance between various pieces of high ground. Sometimes it was a few meters and at other points it might be several thousand. In between lay the abandoned rice paddies and orchards with the unpruned trees still bearing fruit in season.

Korea is not the ugly country painted by war correspondents and footsore troops. Their writings reflect the miseries under which they were forced to live. In spring, the Korean hillsides are ablaze with the colors of dark pink azaleas, purple scabious, poppies and large blue daisies and yellow cineraria. Add to these the mulberry, apple and plum orchards and green seas of the rice paddies and the picture is one of beauty. Many a Marine will remember the fruit from the orchard between the MLH and Marilyn, but won't remember the beauty of the view from Marilyn's crest across the long sweep of valley past Three Fingers and the Claw. Their view was clouded, no doubt, by the vicious little fighters from China who occupied these tracts.

With luck, aggressive patrolling and the utilization of every supporting arm, it could be expected that a reinforced battalion of Marines would hold this over-long line from Bunker to COP 2. However, something had to be done or the enemy would capture COP 2 and other key outposts with their so called "creeping offensive."

By using the No Fire Circle of Panmunjom as a shield, they would dig around COP 2 and cut the road to the corridor. This narrow, rutty affair was the only way to supply the garrison. Once isolated, the outpost would fall from lack of food, water and ammunition. In a siege, water would be of prime importance for there were no natural sources or storage facilities.

To cut this road and isolate the garrison, the Chinese began OPERATION DIG. Gathering together a horde of their best pick and shovel wielders, these human moles began to shovel south from the village of Kamon-Dong. In frustration and with anxiety, the Marines watched this trench line spread like an uncoiling snake and there was little they could do to delay or hinder the enemy. In addition to digging, the enemy was in the habit of giving vent to their hate by a sporadic, though fairly heavy, mortar fire from Kamon-Dong. This fire could not be answered by the Marines for fear of dropping a shell in the circle. The Marines were sure the village was also the storage supply base for the sector.

Along with the digging, other things went on that lent an air of unreality to the whole situation. During the day COP 2 Marines saw groups of Oriental civilians just inside the circle, watching the "diggers." They appeared to be a sort of cheering section. There was also a free flow of people from the circle to the trench line and from trenches back to the circle. At night there was singing by the Dragon Lady, a sultry-voiced Chinese girl who knew all the late American tunes. The music relieved the tedium of the night watch and her propaganda talks held more laughs than most comedy routines.

"Best show in Korea," was the consensus.

The Marines watched during the day, listened at night, and the trench line grew longer and longer. Something must be done, but flat trajectory weapons could not be fired. A miss or ricochet would fly into the holy land of the Circle and the truce talks would be called off by a trigger-tempered Nam II. To forestall possible use of mortars, the Chinese bent their digging so close to the circle that it was impossible to fire with these high-angle weapons. At best the mortar is not a precision weapon. The Marine command had one alternative. If the right site could be found, it was the place for the employment of the Recoilless Rifle.

The Recoilless Rifle does not fall into the same awful category as the atomic bomb, but it comes from the same developing agency — World War II. And it can be as deadly within its sphere of influence. The end result is the same to the man who gets a direct hit.

The Recoilless Rifle is a specialized weapon. It is an artillery piece without wheels; it is an antitank weapon; it can be carried by four men, three if they're willing and able. It can throw a 75 mm. shell several thousand yards with precision. In the vernacular of the troops, the weapon is called a "reckless" rifle. This name stems partly from a contraction of its true name and partly from the fact that one has to be a little on the reckless side to associate with such a weapon. Due to the horrific back blast, it is impossible to conceal its firing position and the enemy is committed to taking instant counteraction.

The RR platoon is a unit in a Marine antitank company and it is under the control of the regimental commander. This arrangement makes them military gypsies in that they may be assigned on a day by day, or even hour to hour basis to one of the three infantry battalions. They are sent wherever the need is most urgent.

At this juncture the 1st Battalion 5th Marines, commanded by Lt. Col. Alexander Gentleman, occupied the Bunker-COP 2 sector. This creeping, digging type of enemy offensive, though slow, could be deadly and Gentleman knew something had to be done to stop it. When observers reported a deep trench through which hand carts of supplies were being moved from Kamon-dong to outlying points, the Marine commander took action.

Gentleman made a reconnaissance with Lt. Eric Pedersen, who commanded the Recoilless Rifle Platoon. It was decided to set up a gun at the confluence of the neutral corridor and the No Fire Circle. From this position the gun could fire into Kamon-dong and the trench works without danger of violating the sanctity of the corridor or the circle. At the same time, it would be virtually impossible for the enemy to return the fire without dropping a shell into the circle or onto the corridor.

If the Chinese should send an infantry force to capture the weapon, all that had to be done was to withdraw a few meters into the corridor, wave the attackers farewell or make gestures even more expressive and understood in all languages. This synthetic, restrictive war around COP 2 was real enough to the Marines who got hurt there, but to those untouched it became a few months of wonderment in their lives.

As soon as Gentleman and Pedersen came to a decision, the younger officer guided a gun squad into position. The circle was three yards to the left and the corridor three to the rear. Sgt. William Cox got the gun set in. With studied exactness Pedersen pointed out the targets in relation to the circle. While this was going on a number of unfriendly civilians and a few in uniform gathered at the edge of the circle to watch the Marines. They did not like what they saw. They shouted, they spat, they threw rocks. Pedersen and his Marines went about the job of getting set in and ignored the hostile spectators.

Cox sighted in on the first house to the right of Kamon-dong. The range was five hundred meters. The first shot had little apparent effect. It disappeared like a drop of water in a dry sponge. The horrendous back blast scattered the irate North Koreans and their anger increased with the sudden fright received. More rocks and insults were hurled at the gun crew. On the second shot a haze of yellow dust blossomed; on the third, the roof fell in and figures were seen pouring from the buildings. Methodically, Cox went about the task of knocking down the mud huts, one by one, from right to left.

The supply of ammunition for the rifle came from an ASP (Ammunition Supply Point) on COP 2. Although ammunition could have been hauled by jeep to within a few yards of the gun by using the corridor, this was against the rules. This meant the carriers in the squad had to man-pack the 75 mm. rounds a distance of nine hundred meters.

The ASP was in defilade on the southern extremity of the outpost. Upon shouldering four rounds (twenty-four pounds each), the ammunition carrier passed through a gate in the wire and for two hundred yards moved down the rutted road leading to the corridor. At this point he turned hard right and, crawling under more wire, gained a rice paddy dike. Somewhat like a tightrope walker, he negotiated this narrow, uneven pathway.

At this juncture he was in view of the enemy, five or six hundred yards on his right hand. His sole protection was the corridor some five hundred yards to the left. If the enemy should shoot and make a hit, all was well, but if the shot missed and went flying over the holy land, the truce negotiators might argue the matter for days. The Chinese were meticulous in observing the rules of this strange warfare and seldom risked a violation.

The threat was there, however, and the Marines sweat it out as they walked the paddy dike. Four hundred yards of dike and then a seven-foot ditch with more wire on the far side. Then came a steep climb to a razor-backed ridge.

After a rough passage through brush and second growth trees where crisp autumn leaves lay on the ground and the sounds were old and cranky as the tired Marines shuffled through them, finally the gun position was reached. Cox was laying in three rounds a minute, so it was necessary to unload hurriedly and double back to the ASP. The project was geared to the idea of doing the job well and quickly and retiring. Despite the risk of violating the corridor, the Chinese would not let the Reckless Rifle perch on Molar and destroy their housing and hard-dug trench line without retaliation of some sort.

It was a panting job for the ammunition carriers. PFC Coleman, six foot three and weighing over two hundred, could shoulder the one hundred eight-pound load with more ease and speed than could his mate, PFC Jose Cordova. For Cordova the weight of the shells was within thirty pounds of his own.

Then Cox hit pay dirt as one of his shots set off an explosion. The village became covered by dust and smoke and the spectators danced with rage.

The Marines unshipped the weapon and carried it into the corridor. Kamon-dong, for the time, was finished as a supply point.

One compensation for being a Reckless "cannoneer" was that the weapon was designed solely for daylight employment. This meant the Reckless crew could spend the nights in some comfort behind the lines. Pedersen had an exhausted crew. No matter how tough they were, the men could not take long, fast hauls over extended periods. As he rode back to their base camp near Changdan, he thought over the problem.

That night he asked Gunnery Sergeant Norman Mull, Platoon Sergeant Joe Latham and Scout Sergeant Willard Berry to his tent.

"We need a horse or a mule to pack ammunition." All nodded in agreement. "A horse could carry eight to ten rounds at a faster pace than a man can carry three." Again the men nodded. "I'll see if I can get permission."

Putting the pack before the horse, Pedersen wrote to his wife Katherine in Vista, California.

"I need a pack saddle! Please get together with Chess and find a good used pack saddle if possible. I don't know how you will be able to send it to me but you'll undoubtedly find a way."

Pedersen drove to the 1st Battalion CP where he found Gentleman in the COG Bunker.

"Kamon-dong is still burning, Pete," the battalion commander greeted him. "That was bloody good shooting today."

"Thank you, Colonel." Pedersen accepted the proffered cup of coffee. "Running that ammunition over rice paddies just about whipped the squad though. I'd like to get a horse. Will you back me on it?"

"Sure. I'll do more than that. I'll let you borrow a one-ton trailer to haul it around. I'll also call Jess Ferrill and tell him I think it's a great idea. But where are you going to get a horse?"

"I thought I'd go to the race track in Seoul. There ought to be some horses for sale around there."

Pedersen's company commander, Captain Henry Checklou, was neither opposed nor enthusiastic over the idea. Checklou could see more value in the horse as a mascot than as an ammunition carrier. He finally agreed to approach the regimental commander on the subject. The RR Platoon heard of the project and were tumultuous in their approval. Every man volunteered to act as groom.

The next morning, after the regimental briefing, Checklou found the opportunity to speak with Col. Eustace P, Smoak, commanding officer of the 5th Marines.

Checklou said, "Colonel, some of the men in my unit would like permission to have a mascot."

Smoak was surprised at this request inasmuch as the regiment was already well filled with mascot dogs. Marines are noted for their love of children and dogs and liberty. Though there were orders against it, certain rear area units had Korean orphans living with them. On inspection days these children took to the hills and sat it out until it was safe to return.

"I don't see why you shouldn't have a mascot, Henry. What do you have in mind?"

Checklou cleared his throat. "A horse, sir."

"A horse!" Smoak stared at the company commander. "A horse for a mascot?"

Smoak's executive officer, Lt. Col. Jess Ferrill, spoke up, "Al Gentleman called last night. He thinks it's a good idea."

"It would be more than just a mascot, Colonel. The Reckless Rifle Platoon want a horse to carry ammunition. Being mascot would be additional duty, sort of."

"Okay, Henry, get your mascot. The next time I'm in your area, I'll drop by to have a look at it."

Early the following morning Corporal Philip Carter drove his jeep with borrowed trailer attached, to Pedersen's tent. Pedersen and Scout Sgt. Willard Berry were waiting. Berry crawled into the back seat and Pedersen climbed stiffly in beside Carter. The young officer was hampered by leg and thigh wounds received a short time before.

The trip south from Changdan along the corridor road to Freedom Bridge, crossing the Imjim River (a dark coil of putrid water) and as far as Munsan-ni, was pleasant. The Army engineers had worked over this section to smooth the way for the truce negotiators who had to make daily trips into Panmunjom. Once south of the negotiator's village, the road quickly fell apart — too much and too heavy military traffic for a road designed for horse carts.

The road ran past burned-out hamlets, broken houses, flattened orchards, barren paddies, all sadly ruined by war. Thirty-five miles of jolting and they came to Seoul. They entered the city through the north gate, or what had once been the entrance to a walled city.

Poor, battered Seoul. Fought over by invader and friendly rescuer and damaged as much by one as the other. At one time Seoul had been a clean, rather comely Oriental city. Now the red tile of its homes lay in rubble in the streets and everywhere there were spaces where only the shells of buildings remained. On a few of the main streets the streetcars just barley ran and on the narrow, ancient secondary streets there roamed scavenger dogs and hungry, homeless people.

Everywhere there were these little stalls, hopelessly shabby and dust-covered with the keepers in a trance of hunger and despair except for their dark eyes that watched and watched. To Pedersen and his fellow Marines there was nothing quite so sad as the starving shopkeepers who must choose between replacing the stock or using money from a sale to buy food.

They drove to the headquarters of the Army Purchasing Mission. Pedersen spoke with a lieutenant of the Quartermaster Corps. The army man knew of no horses or mules for sale.

"Why don't you try the race track? It's being used as an Army OY and helicopter strip, but there are still some Korean horses housed there. Try the track."

He leaned against the jeep and spoke to Carter. "It's not far. Follow this street, Hae-Wha-Dong, south until you come to streetcar tracks. That's Chong-Ro or Big Bell Road. Turn left and follow the tracks about two miles and you'll see the race course on your right. Used to be quite a place. They tell me there'd be a hundred thousand people there on a big day."

They found the track without difficulty and drove into the stable area. They were greeted by a young, smiling Korean. He spoke English after a fashion. Pedersen made his wants known as other natives gathered.

The Korean asked, "You pay hwan or dooler?"

Pedersen knew it was against regulations to use U.S. currency, but he didn't know where to exchange his money. He answered, "American dollars."

The Korean smiled and led the way to a stall, Pedersen saw a thin, scabious animal with harness sores. He shook his head and moved on. The next horse was better, but not pleasing. A third and fourth followed. At the fifth stall he looked over the half door. Quickly he stepped inside with the voluble Korean at his heels.

The Marine studied the little red filly; he noted her three white stockings, the blaze, the intelligent eye and fine head. He remembered a horse he had once owned as a youth in Arizona. This was even better, far better.

He put out his hand and she accepted it without alarm. The hair was fine and the skin smooth underneath. Pedersen thought of his children in California. How they would love her! He spread her lips and looked at the eye tooth.

"How old?" he asked.

"Four years and three months." The Korean grinned, "By your counting."

"How much?"

"How much you pay?"

"One hundred fifty dollars." Pedersen held up a forefinger and then bent it double.

His guide looked pained. "This is the best horse in Chosen." Forgetting himself, the Korean lapsed into his native tongue and recounted the animal's history. He ended in English, "No, no! Not enough."

Pedersen made up his mind not to haggle. He said firmly, "I will pay two hundred fifty dollars. That is all I have and that is all I will pay."

He knew he had impressed the man. The fellow turned and shouted. For the first time Pedersen saw a Korean standing some distance from the stall. There was a volley of words back and forth. The guide turned.

"My friend will sell. Please leave the stall for him to say his sayonara."

The Marines were surprised at the ease with which the little horse accepted the smallness of the trailer. Bolstering the sides with bamboo staffs for support, Carter drove away.

Berry leaned forward. "Lieutenant, it looked to me as though that Korean wanted to cry. He liked this pony."

Balancing herself on the precarious platform of a jeep trailer, Flame rode into a new life. It was dark when the jeep pulled into the Changdan camp, but the RR Platoon broke out of their tents to greet the recruit. The choice of a companion was important and the young officer had given the matter considerable thought on the ride back from Seoul. He finally decided on PFC Monroe Coleman, a large, soft-spoken youth with a lifetime background of ranch life in Utah. This seemed to fit him to be consort for the little mare.

Pedersen asked Coleman, "How'd you like the job of taking care of her?"

Coleman grinned, "I'd sure like to, sir. I like horses."

"Good." Pedersen turned to Platoon Sergeant Latham. "She'll not be ridden by anyone at any time. In the morning we'll build a bunker for her."

Latham, an Alabaman with years' experience around horses, ran his hand along Flame's neck. "When I was stationed at Pensacola we had a twelve-horse stable for base patrol."

"Okay, Joe, you're the D.I. Put her through boot camp."

"Shouldn't it be hoof camp, Lieutenant?"

"Guess you're right."

"What's her name?"

"I don't know—"

From the darkness a voice said, "Reckless. Let's call her Reckless."

There was immediate approval. No horse feed being available, Reckless was taken to the mess tent. Her first Marine meal consisted of a loaf of bread and uncooked oatmeal.

In due course, Kay Pedersen received the letter asking for a pack saddle. She took the problem to her father, Arthur Wells, vice-president of the San Diego Trust and Savings Bank. Together they called on an old friend, Dr. Robert Immenschuh, a local veterinarian. The problem was solved then and there as Immenschuh donated a pack saddle to the cause.

Next came the difficulty of getting such a bulky bundle accepted for air mail. Postal regulations on service air mail was limited to two pounds and a package not over thirty inches in length and girth. The pack weighed forty pounds and would fill a mail sack. Fortunately a friendly, understanding mail clerk closed his eyes to the regulations and accepted the saddle. The Reckless Rifle Platoon of the 5th Marines had a horse and the pack saddle was on its way.

CHAPTER II

IT WAS GETTING COLDER and it took some prodding to get the Marines to crawl from their blankets in the morning. Korean sparrows headed south to become Japanese sparrows for the winter. The Marines watched duck formations vee across the sky and those in jobs detached from contact with the enemy, took to the fields for pheasant and duck shooting. Occasionally the more daring helicopter pilots would fan low over a startled deer while a crew mate shot it. Such hunting was unsportsmanlike, but it did bring fresh meat to the mess.

Supply officers saw to the distribution of long-handled underwear and stoves were set up in tents and bunkers. It was a new type of military stove developed during the war in Korea. They were humorous-looking things — round, pot-bellied, with a Puckish look about them. They would burn nearly any kind of fuel and their feeding was simple. Outside the tent or bunker was a barrel of fuel and from this ran a rubber hose, garter-snake size, which fitted its mouth to a carburetor. An adjustment knob would feed fuel onto the flame at the rate desired. If properly cared for they were safe and efficient. If neglected, they were smelly, temperamental and as quick to overheat as an angry Frenchman.

No civilians were allowed north of the Imjim River. Their villages and remains of villages were there, but the military was freed from the worry of being hampered by helpless noncombatants. For the most part, the hutches left behind were of brown mud walls with plaited rice straw roofs, now mildewed black. Wretched hovels, grim and deserted; it was difficult to imagine people living in them.

The area about Changdan was different. The houses and public buildings were of stone and had been, at one time, substantial. During the period of Japanese occupation the area was used as a hunting preserve by the wealthy from Seoul. It was a rich countryside with a fine yearly yield of rice, kaoliang, barley and various fruits. Modern history does not record a crop failure in this district.

Changdan was the site of the battalion command post defending the line from Outpost Bunker to COP-2. Masked from the enemy by rugged, lofty Mill 229, the village lay in a fertile valley. The stone houses had been badly battered and few were habitable. The concrete and mortar shell of the bank with its iron safe opened and rusted was a constant reminder to the Marines that a well-to-do rural people had once been in Changdan. The safe door was left open on order, to restrain the curious from probing about. Even with the door open, it was a magnet to Marines. The battalion staff lived in tents and bunkers. Though within range of enemy artillery and mortars, the enemy were more prone to fire on targets within their vision than to gamble on the chance of a lucky, blind hit behind Hill 229.

The Recoilless Rifle Platoon had established its camp south of Changdan and facing on the road leading to the corridor. The day following Flame's arrival was a busy one. Besides fulfilling their commitments for fire missions on the front, there was a bunker to build and horse feed to be purchased. The Chinese appeared to be stunned by the unexpected bombardment of Kamon-dong, which was still burning, and there were no calls for more shelling from Gentleman. The rest of the front was quiet, so Pedersen was free to make arrangements for his recruit.

The platoon turned to, to build a bunker and fence in a small pasture. While this was going on, Latham went south of the Imjim to buy feed. A shoebrush was dug out of a sea bag and the little horse was thoroughly gone over. There were many volunteer hands to supplement Coleman's and her coat took on the sheen of a Marine dress boot. The shoe polish on the brush may have added to the luster.

Flame accepted the new surroundings and many hands calmly. She had never had so much food nor such a varied diet. For the first time in her life she ate an apple, many of them. Carrots also were new. And her mouth salivated over her first Hershey bar. That afternoon when the wire was up and Coleman turned her loose, she romped in sheer exuberance from so much attention and food. In pure vanity she went into her rocking horse gait and there were loud huzzahs from the audience. That spurred her to greater efforts. Finally she tired of showing off and, going to a far corner, began to nibble at the grass. It was the first such food she had had since becoming a Marine.

The Marines were reluctant to turn to the more arduous task of sandbagging the roof of the bunker. The protective abode was being built to specifications laid down by the division engineer for all bunkers; beams and crossbeams of certain size with a minimum of four feet of sandbags on the roof. Such an overhead, it was estimated, would stop any shell the Chinese might throw over the hill.

The peacefulness of the scene was broken when two mascot dogs from the Tank Platoon roamed into the pasture on a friendly, sniffing mission. Flame saw them and went into a tantrum. With ears flattened and teeth bared, she went slashing at them. The startled Marines dropped their tools and went running to their friend. The dogs ran screaming from the pasture and didn't stop until they were crouched under the protection of a friendly Pershing tank a half mile away.

The platoon gathered around Flame. Her eyes flashed a white rim and she trembled. Coleman tried to console her.

"Easy, Reckless, take it easy, little horse." He ran a gentle hand along her neck. "Guess she doesn't like dogs."

"That is the understatement of this war, Coleman," Staff Sergeant Pat O'Rourke observed.

George "Doc" Mitchell, naval hospital corpsman, offered a medical opinion. "Acts like she was scared as a kid by a dog. Has a psychosis probably. Better pass the word to keep dogs away from her."

Under the sedative of an apple, Reckless quieted and was introduced to her new home about the time Latham drove into the pasture with a trailer filled with barley, sorghum and rice straw. A liberal bed of straw was placed on the deck and a Marine green blanket came from one of the bunks as a night sleepcoat.

Pedersen and Sgt. Berry, who had been on a mission scouting out new gun positions, returned to camp. The officer inspected Reckless' bedroom. Except for putting a tarpaulin across the door, it was complete. Pedersen expressed his pleasure with the arrangement, but Cordova was not completely satisfied.

"Mr. Pedersen, this aint goin' to be warm enough, come winter. These Korean winters will freeze the —"

"When it gets that cold, Cordova," Latham interrupted, "I'll take her into my tent and let her sleep by my stove."

Reckless accepted the new life in stride. Her curiosity took her to every corner of the barbed-wire enclosure. She found the galley tent and one morning PFC Billy Jones, a recent arrival, offered her a plate of scrambled eggs. She ate with relish and showed even greater appetite for the coffee that followed.

This discovery delayed breakfast and Cordova warned Jones, "Wait'll Reckless finds out you've been feedin' her powdered eggs. She'll chase you over the hill like she did those dogs."

Thereafter she made periodic visits to the galley and came to eat more and more food from that source. Her eagerness to learn Marine ways led her into tents where her friends lived. After the first few days she was no longer tied in the bunker, but allowed to roam. On nights when she couldn't sleep, she would visit various tents. If she showed an inclination to stay on after "lights out," it was no task to realign sleeping bags to make room.

At the request of the platoon, Gentleman asked his battalion surgeon to drop by and examine the recruit. He certified her "physically fit and capable of performing the duties of a Marine of her age and rank."

Latham was hindered in his recruit training program until the pack saddle arrived from California. While waiting, there were things that could be done. There was the daily practice of getting into and out of a trailer. In no time she became as nimble as any Marine going on a liberty run. There were walks in the hills and the teaching of caution on coming to wire. She showed a sensitivity to barbed wire and her passage through it was never without fear.

When faced with strange circumstances, she would lower her head and look over the situation carefully. Her fear of the wire made the air whistle from her nostrils and this gave the appearance of "smelling out" the danger. After she had given an obstacle a close once-over, she would proceed anywhere a friendly guide might ask.

When Latham and the recruit had become thoroughly acquainted and a close bond established, the training became more detailed. Latham taught her to lie down.

"This," he explained, "would come in handy if Reckless were ever caught under fire where there was no cover." He also taught her to kneel in case sometime it might be necessary for her to crawl into a shallow bunker. As a joke on the platoon and Doc Mitchell in particular, he got the little sorrel to limp painfully on her right front leg whenever he flicked it with a switch. Until Mitchell caught on to the trick, he was all for taking Reckless to the hospital ship. Never in his fourteen years in the Corps had Latham worked so diligently with a recruit.

Reckless took all this in good humor. On her own she developed several pranks to amuse herself and rankle Latham. There were times when she would not allow him to catch her. She would continue to feed with studied unconcern as he approached, but when he was three or four feet from her, she would snort and rear in mock alarm and race away. She would circle, at her rocking horse gait, then charge her pursuer with ears back and teeth bared. At the last moment she would skid to a stop, rear, and with front hoofs flashing, spin away for another run. After a time of this tomfoolery, she would walk directly to him and ask for candy.

Latham was happy to announce to Pedersen and the world, "Tell her what you want and let her look the situation over an' she'll do it, if she's with someone she trusts."

No matter the worthiness of a project, there will always be detractors, motivated mostly by jealousy. In the case of Reckless this was true. When she first appeared in the Recoilless Rifle camp, Marines from other units came to see her. They were impressed with her beauty and the glowing reports of her deportment in "hoof" camp. There was little that could be said against her, so the indirect method of criticism was used.

"Been under fire yet?"

"Nope."

"Been around the Reckless Rifle when it was fired?"

"Nope."

A long face and pursing of lips at this. "Well, you know how it is with horses. They never learn to take heavy fire. Mules will. Horses won't. That's why they used mules in World War I. Horses are too flighty, go crazy under fire."

"You don't know Reckless, Mac."

"I know horses. Just wait'll she's on the line some day and little China-boy starts dropping incoming." A derisive laugh. "Your horse will be outgoing."

Though the talk of these detractors was discounted, there was planted a sneaking, undernourished doubt. The back blast of a recoilless rifle is a scorching, grass-tearing, pebble-tossing thing. It is the nature of the weapon. A 75 mm. Pack Howitzer or a French 75 recoils with terrific force. This recoil is absorbed and controlled by an intricate system of oils under hydromatic pressure. The recoilless rifle firing the same size shell has no such system and the expanding gases escape in an explosive belch that is not only noisy but dangerous to anyone standing behind the weapon.

Latham ignored the itch of fear he felt under his left shoulder blade and took Reckless for an inspection of the weapon. She explored the length of the barrel and lost interest.

"Its bark is worse than its bite," he told her, "unless you're standing directly behind it, there's no danger."

One day there was a flurry of excitement as a jeep rolled into camp. On the front bumper there was a red sign bearing two stars. Major General Edwin Pollock, commanding general of the 1st Marine Division, had dropped in to meet the newest recruit to his command.

Reckless was looking her best. Coleman had just given her a good brushing and her coat shone in the morning sun. The general went over her with an experienced hand and practiced eye. He was pleased with what he saw.

It must be admitted that Reckless was not too impressed by her visitor. At this point in her Marine career two silver stars on a collar meant no more than two stripes on a sleeve. She could feel the excitement in Coleman, however, so she remained quiet.

"When are you to start using her to carry ammunition?" the general asked Pedersen.

"As soon as the pack arrives, sir. It shouldn't be long. I've had a letter from my wife telling me it's on the way."

The general looked at each hoof in turn. "She needs new shoes."

"Yes, sir. My platoon sergeant is south of the Imjim now looking for a native horseshoer."

"Let me know if you don't find one."

"Yes, sir."

Latham returned without having found a horseshoer. Later in the day, Lt. Eugene Foxworth, the general's aide, called Pedersen on the telephone. A Korean blacksmith had been found in a village not far from the division CP. The next day Latham loaded his recruit into the trailer and drove to the village, as directed by Foxworth. He found the Korean, who was eager to earn his fee. He spoke to Reckless in Korean. Apparently she understood the words, but did not much like his hand.

Latham followed the two into a small hut where the horseshoer tied Reckless to a center pole. The fellow was brusque and rough. When he tried to look at her feet, she would have none of him. The cobbler yanked her head around and snubbed her closer.

Latham said sharply, "Take it easy, Mac!"

The man smiled. He brought out a chain with which he was going to tie her down. This was too much. Reckless began to rear and kick. The cobbler flew out the door. As Latham rushed to her side to calm her the center pole gave way and crashed down on his head. He fell to the floor stunned.

When he crawled from under the debris the Korean was sitting to one side, nursing his bruises. The hut was a wreck. When she saw Latham emerge, she walked directly to him. He loaded her into the trailer and they returned to Changdan.

That night the Marines sat around and talked of Reckless and laughed over the way she had kicked the Korean blacksmith out of the hutch. And it might be said the story lost no facet of glitter in the polishing. They were proud of her and hoped, desperately, they could stay proud of her when she first came under enemy fire.

Latham did what he could to trim her feet and tighten her shoes. If Reckless would have nothing to do with local cobblers, she would have to wait until there was time to drive into Seoul. There must be someone at her old home on the race track who could handle her.

The pack saddle arrived from California and serious work began. After experimenting and making certain adaptations, it was found that six rounds were the simplest load to secure. That number did not appear to burden Reckless unduly. With adjustments, eight and ten rounds could be carried, but Pedersen ruled such a load would only be carried in the most urgent situations. Reckless accepted the pack and load without qualm or protest and appeared to delight in roaming the hills with her friends.

After one particularly difficult trial run, the return to camp was made as the truck arrived from the Division PX. On a sudden inspiration, Latham poured a coca cola into helmet. Reckless drank it thirstily, eagerly. She nuzzled for more when it was gone.

"Hey! D'ja see that? Reckless likes coke."

"What's so funny about that? She likes anything we've given her so far."

"Better not give her any more until we check with the doctor."

Doc Mitchell considered the question. "Not more'n a couple of bottles a day. The carbonated water might not be good for her kidneys."

The platoon was assigned a fire mission into Hedy's Crotch. The company facing on this sector had detected trenches being dug. The Recoilless Rifles would delay the enemy building program. It was decided that Reckless was ready for her baptism of fire.

The distance from Changdan to the shooting site was two and a half miles. The first portion of the way was shielded by the spine of hills which run eastward from Hill 229. At the destroyed hamlet of Kwakchon a turn to the north led onto a road that was narrow and rutted. A portion of this was navigable. The final five hundred yards to the ridge line was a steep, breathtaking drag on foot.

Of further interest to the move into firing positions was a six-hundred-yard portion of the so-called road north of Kwakchon. This section was under enemy observation from towering Yoke. Depending on the Chinese mood of the moment, the road was brought under fire when the enemy observers saw too much traffic moving northward on it. While not many hits were recorded, the passage over this stretch did lend a degree of anticipatory breathlessness.

Pedersen spaced his vehicles at ten minute intervals so as not to alarm the trigger-fingered enemy. The first vehicle carried the weapon and the squad, the next bore Reckless and her trailer, while the last brought the ammunition. The passage of the exposed road was made without incident. Sergeant Ralph Sherman and his gun crew began the stiff climb with the heavy weapon.

Reckless scrambled from the trailer and nudged Latham for a piece of chocolate.

"No pogey bait 'til this is over," he told her. Six rounds of high explosive (HE) were secured to the pack and Latham gave her a slap of encouragement. "Okay, Reckless, we'll soon know if you're a Marine or a mouse."

"She ain't going to get shook, Sarge," Coleman promised. He took the lead rope in hand and began the climb. They soon overtook the gun crew, Sherman directed Coleman to off-load at the first firing position and to return to the truck for another load. Pedersen and Berry had preceded the party and were on the ridge line searching out targets with the infantry commander.

Experience had shown it took from four to six minutes for the enemy to react to a sighting and begin counterfire. The tactic of the gun crew was fire and movement. When the gun was set in and target established, the weapon would be fired four to five times. This was done with speed and precision. Then the weapon was displaced to a new position while enemy counterfire fell in the area of the recently abandoned site. This procedure would be followed from second, third and fourth firing seat. Hopscotch shooting of this nature continued until the mission was deemed accomplished.

It was only natural the Marine infantry manning the line did not cheer the appearance of a reckless gun crew. It meant they would be recipients of

incoming thrown at the telltale dust and smoke of the weapon's back blast. It was a dividend of Chinese hate the infantrymen would rather not receive. Sometime, by ill luck, the enemy did guess the maneuver correctly, with tragic results to the gun crew. It was only when they had the protection of the corridor and holy circle of Panmunjom that they could sit still and shoot it out.

Speed and teamwork were the key to a successful shoot. It was breathless, scrambling work over the difficult terrain and in the excitement of the moment the little red horse was forgotten. Coleman had delivered his first load and was returning with the second when Sherman opened fire.

"Wham-whoosh!" the hills bellowed and rocketed with the roar. Behind the weapon spurted a flume of dust. Though weighted down with six shells, Reckless left the ground with all four feet — her eyes went white.

"Take it easy, Reckless," Coleman begged.

"Wham-whoosh!" Sherman was on target and driving them home.

Reckless went into the air again, but not quite so far. More soft talk from Coleman. She snorted and shook her head to stop the ringing in her ears.

"Wham-whoosh!"

She shook as the concussive blast of air struck her, but she did not rear. She stood closer to Coleman, trembling slightly, but the white was gone from her eyes. She began to take an interest in the actions of the gun crew.

"Wham-whoosh!" Her reaction was little more than a jerk of her head.

"Let's go!" Guido, the section leader, shouted. It was time to displace the weapon.

With the precision of a professional quarterback, Sherman directed his gun crew. The shift to the new position was made with Reckless and Coleman at their heels. The six rounds she carried were off-loaded and down the steep hill the pair went for another load. Enemy incoming, a site behind, began to blast and rocket on the ridge line. This new diversion caused her to sweat more than the climb and load warranted. A thin line of lather showed under the pack straps.

Latham joined them. He ran his hand down her wet neck. "You're all right, Reckless." She rubbed against him and he roughed her about the ears. This took her mind from the roar of the gun and the blast of incoming and she calmed.

Five times Reckless and Coleman negotiated the rugged hillside with ammunition. During the last series of shots she stood a short distance from the gun picking around in the sparse grass for something edible.

The weapon was displaced into defiladed position down the hillside. For the first time the gun crew had an opportunity to consider the deportment of their friend.

"How'd she do, Coleman?" Guido asked.

"The first couple of times she took off, straight up. I'll bet she went eight feet into the air on the first one. After that she got used to it."

"What about the incoming?"

"Made her sweat some."

"Who doesn't sweat?"

"On that last firing position," Latham told them, "she wasn't more'n forty feet away when you fired. Know what she was doing? She was tryin' to eat an old helmet liner she found in a hole."

"Where's that character and all his mule talk? We'll make him eat those words."

"Make him eat the mule."

Reckless rode back to camp in high style. Because the day had turned warm and the hill so steep, Latham offered her a can of beer. She drank it and asked for more.

That night it rained. A cold, sweeping rain of late December. Though Reckless' bunker was rain proof, she became restless. Perhaps her ears still rang from the blasting of the rifle. She left her bunker and made her way into the staff NCO tent. Latham, O'Rourke and Mull greeted her warmly. Latham wiped her dry and covered her with a blanket. In no time at all was in a head-nodding sleep beside the stove. She was one of them. She was a Marine who had been under enemy fire.

CHAPTER III

THE PLATOON lost a friend when Gentleman was transferred to the division staff, but gained a new one with the arrival of Lt. Col. Edwin Wheeler to command the First. The aggressive tactics of carrying the war to the enemy went unchanged. There were periodic shellings of Kamondong and the trenches nearby; there were missions to fire in and about Hedy, and there was always Bunker. Besides the targets in the First Battalion sector, there were equally lucrative ones to the right where the Second Battalion faced on outposts Reno, Carson and Vegas. So the men of the platoon and their horse roved the line from Panmunjom to the Samchon River.

Late in November the request came through for another shoot into enemy positions from Bunker. This was always a nervy assignment in that the enemy reacted with greater alacrity and fierceness than anywhere else along the line.

Gentleman had reasoned, "Luke is mighty touchy around Bunker. He doesn't like it when we shoot him up. Whenever you find something he doesn't like, keep giving it to him."

Wheeler adopted this policy. Pedersen chose section leader Guido and Sherman's squad to make the shoot. To reach Bunker, which was four hundred meters in front of the line, entailed the usual passage through wire and some stiff climbing. Pedersen decided to leave Reckless behind on this occasion mainly because of the wire. Bunker was situated on a rugged land mass that also held Hedy five hundred meters to the southwest. From this outpost named for the historic battleground, the Marines could look into the valleys behind glowering Yoke — and the Chinese always were sensitive to having people look into their backyards.

Guido and Sherman got the gun set in and Pedersen selected the target. The tactic of fire and movement was begun. Enemy reaction was more fierce than usual. Incoming began to rain onto the ridge line. The Chinese made no attempt at precision counter battery fire, but blanketed the whole area. Pedersen was wounded in the hip and leg by a near mortar blast. Wheeler called off the fire mission and the squad assisted their leader back to the main line and into the battalion aid station. Pedersen had his wounds dressed, but refused evacuation. Late in the afternoon he rejoined the unit at Changdan.

Each evening at 7:00 there is a briefing in the division CP. At such meetings various members of the General's staff recount the activities of his section for the preceding twenty-four hours. On this evening Colonel Russell Honsowetz, division operations officer, described the action on Bunker. He concluded that portion of his report by saying, "The enemy appeared to be more sensitive than usual in the Bunker area. His counterfire was accurate and intense. Lt. Pedersen, the Recoilless Rifle Platoon leader, was wounded."

Later in the briefing when Colonel Sidney Kelly reported on personnel, he informed Pollock, "This is the third wound for Pedersen."

The General's reaction was as spontaneous as that of the Chinese earlier in the day. He told Kelly, "Get him out of there. Transfer him out of combat."

After the briefing, Kelly telephoned Smoak. "The General wants Pedersen of your antitank company transferred out of combat. Send him up here for reassignment."

Checklou notified Pedersen that he was being relieved and to report to regiment in the morning. Unaware of what had transpired at the division briefing, the young troop commander spent a worrisome night. His wounds, still in the throbbing stage, caused further distress.

This meant a double loss to the platoon. They would not only lose an officer whom they respected, but they would also lose Reckless. Of the two it must be admitted the loss of the horse was the greater. Another Marine officer would replace Pedersen; perhaps he would not have Pedersen's skill and temperament, but good or bad, officers could be borne. Life without Reckless was another matter.

A meeting was called by Mull and Latham.

"There's not much we can do about it," Latham explained. "Reckless is his horse. He paid for her. If he wants to take her, we're dead."

Mull added, "The Lieutenant will be fair. He'll think of Reckless and us before he does himself. Here's what we oughta do. Take up a collection and pay him back."

In a short time enough money was collected to repay the officer. From the deep shadows along the tent wall a new thought was voiced, "There's one thing we're forgetting."

"What's that?"

"Reckless. Maybe she'd like to get out of combat too. Did anybody ever think of that?"

"Aw, she likes it up here!"

"If she does, she ought to have her head examined."

The platoon had not considered the mood or character of Pedersen. The young officer had no intention of being relieved of his platoon without taking the matter up with higher authority. He requested and was granted permission to speak with the regimental commander. Colonel Smoak was considerate and impressed, but there was nothing he could do. The order had come down from Division. He gave Pedersen permission to plead his cause with General Pollock.

Pedersen telephoned Major Charles Lamb, division adjutant and an old friend.

He told Lamb, "Charlie, they're trying to transfer me because I got nicked the other day. I think they're treating me like a Boy Scout. All I want to do is stay with my platoon. Can you fix it up so I can see General Pollock?"

Lamb said he would try to arrange a meeting.

Lamb went to the General's van.

"Sir, Lieutenant Eric Pedersen of the 5th Antitank Company has requested permission to see the General."

"What's it about, Charlie?"

"The order transferring him out of combat. Pedersen wants to stay with his platoon." Lamb smiled, "He thinks he's being treated like a Boy Scout."

"He does, eh!" Pollock smiled. "Any of his wounds carried over from the last war?"

"No, sir. All Korean."

"What's his background, Charlie."

"Thirty-two, married and two children. His father was a gun designer. Invented the Pedersen Device which made the old 03 Springfield a semiautomatic weapon. Eric had good schooling — lived in England for a number of years when his father was with the Vickers Company. Spent most of his life in and around Jackson's Hole, Wyoming and Prescott, Arizona. Loves horses."

"I suppose that accounts for Reckless."

"Yes, sir. Eric enlisted in the Marine Corps when he was eighteen; was a captain at the end of World War II. He left the Corps for a time. When, he came back in, the pinch was on and the best he could get was Chief Warrant. Now he's back to first lieutenant."

General Pollock, a veteran of Guadalcanal, Saipan and Iwo Jima, knew the loyalties that build up in a man for a group of men. It was stronger in combat and with small unit commanders. He also knew that, all too often, it was the willing and eager who were killed. He came to a decision.

"Have him in tomorrow morning."

"Yes, sir."

The next morning Lamb ushered his friend into the General's quarters and departed.

"Sir, I request that my orders be changed and that I be allowed to stay with my platoon."

"I think any man who has received three wounds should be taken out of combat. Is there any reason why I should make an exception in your case, Pedersen?"

"None that are sound, sir. I just want to stay with my platoon."

"Reckless have anything to do with this?"

"Yes, sir, in a way. If I leave and take her with me it will be a blow to the platoon. If I leave her behind, it will be a double loss to me — losing her and the platoon."

"All right, Pedersen, return to your platoon. I'll have your orders changed." Pollock smiled, "I don't want my junior officers thinking they're being treated like Boy Scouts."

Pedersen gulped and reddened. "Thank you, sir."

"Thank Reckless. I don't feel like forcing a decision of Solomon on you at this time. By the way, is she as good under fire as I hear she is?"

"Yes, sir. She got used to it a lot quicker than some Marines I know. The first day she might have panicked, but she figured out we knew what we were doing. Nothing shakes her now."

"One of these days we should promote her to corporal. I assume she made PFC in boot camp."

"Yes, sir. My gunnery sergeant says she's qualified for promotion."

"Good. Let me know. If I can get away I'd like to be at the formation."

"Yes, sir."

After Pedersen left, Pollock called Lamb on the telephone. "The 5th Marines are going into reserve in a few days anyway, Charlie, so let Pedersen stay with his outfit for the time."

Pedersen called on Gentleman.

"Hello, Eric. I was expecting you'd drop by. I heard about your being relieved at the briefing last night. Too bad. Your platoon will miss you."

"I just saw the General. He's going to let me stay."

"That's swell, boy. If there's anything I can do to help you, let me know."

"Thanks, Colonel."

Carter was waiting outside Gentleman's tent. Pedersen climbed into the jeep with some difficulty. Carter swung the machine about and headed for Changdan. Before they arrived, the darkness had grown complete and all that could be seen were the two thin lights of the jeep. Carter let Pedersen out and hurried to Latham's tent.

"Mister Pedersen's staying. The general knocked off the transfer."

Latham smiled. "Find Reckless. This deserves a drink. I've been savin' a coke for her."

They found her at the galley having a late snack of half a loaf of bread with strawberry jam. By this rime she had learned to drink from a glass and the coke came at the right time for bread always made her thirsty. Later she went to Latham's tent and dozed by the stove while he wrote letters home.

That night Pedersen wrote his wife:

"So many things have happened to me since I last wrote that I don't know where to start. I was relieved of my platoon and was told to report to Colonel Smoak. I didn't know why and didn't find out until I had seen the Colonel.

"Orders had been issued to remove me from the lines because I had been wounded three times. Col. Smoak couldn't do anything about it so I had to see Gen. Pollock. He let me go back to my platoon! So-o-o, I'm back with my outfit. For a while it looked like I was going to be sent to the 'rear with the gear.'"

PFC Arnold Baker had been assigned second companion to Reckless so that if anything happened to Coleman, he could take over the full duty. A section had been assigned to a mission on the right flank in support of Kurth's Fox Company of the Second. Reckless went along and a temporary pasture was set up for her in a valley known to the Koreans as Hwajon-dong, and was shielded from the enemy by Hill 114. In this particular sector, jeeps and trucks could reach points close to firing sites, so that Reckless was forced into a period of unemployment.

It was during this phase that Baker decided his friend was not getting enough exercise. Conveniently forgetting Pedersen's order against anyone riding her, Baker led her from the pasture and, in the best style of John Wayne, swung onto her back.

From that moment events were blurred as Reckless took off at a full run. Baker tugged on the halter rope and yelled, "Whoa! Reckless, Whoa!" This only spurred her on. He thought of throwing himself from her back and letting her go it alone, but decided against such action when he thought of facing Latham. He twined his fingers in her mane and hung on grimly. Come what might, he was committed to staying with her.

She was a darting shadow crossing the paddy west of the pasture. When she sped by the tank laager and took the road leading to the main line, Baker became frantic. He tugged furiously on the rope.

"Not that way!" Reckless responded with more speed. It was the first good run she had had since joining the Marines and she dug in with an exuberance that made her a red blur in the afternoon light.

To Reckless it was a delightful outing. The road was nearly level with an easy cushion, and the air was fresh and keen. She lengthened her stride as though she would run to Manchuria. Baker groaned. The road chosen by the little horse passed through the barbed wire entanglements at a "gate" from which patrols issued at night. During the day a sentry with a field telephone handy kept watch; at night a squad took positions to permit exit and entry of patrols. Beyond the gate were the fruit orchards and flowers of a lush countryside; shortly north of the orchards lay the minefields through which ran narrow, prescribed lanes for the patrols. Safe passageways to the knowing and wary, but dangerous to the heedless.

Just warming to her run, Reckless flashed through the gate. The sentry let out a yell and cranked on the telephone: "Reckless is loose! She's through the gate an' heading for Unggok —"

Passing the orchard the road was downhill and Reckless approached the speed of sound as she swept into the paddy land between outposts Ava and Corinne. The lookouts on Hill 120, on Ava and Corinne reported her flashing progress. Doubtlessly, the Chinese on mighty, towering Taedok-Song saw her, too, and wondered what Marine trick this might be.

Latham heard and bounded into a jeep and was away on a snarl of tires.

High above and six hundred meters to the east the Marines of Fox Company saw her. They began to shout in desperation.

"Go back, Reckless! Go back."

"Let's shoot in front of her, maybe that'll turn her."

"Too dangerous."

"Who's that on her?"

"Can't make him out."

"Wait'll Latham gets hold of him."

Then, as though enough running was enough, Reckless made a gentle looping turn in the minefield while half a thousand Marines watched and prayed. A long sigh like a spring wind in the trees passed the length of the line as the little horse galloped back past the orchard and through the gate.

Blowing nicely and in a fine sweat, she swept along until meeting up with Latham. With ears pricking and eyes aglow she went to her friend and told him what a great run she had just had. Ashen-faced and limp, Baker slid from her back.

Marine platoon sergeants have their own way of taking care of thoughtless young men who disobey orders.

The 5th Marines were relieved and moved into positions in division reserve. It grew colder and there was snow, but not nearly so much as the winter before when the Marines had been on the eastern front. Reckless grew a heavier coat and it came out more chestnut than sorrel. While there was no ammunition to carry, there was a new job of stringing communication wire. With reels of wire on her pack, she could string more telephone wire in a day than ten Marines.

Being in division reserve meant that the 1st and 5th Regiments were in the line and the 5th in positions where either line regiment could be reinforced in case of need. It also meant a relaxing of tension and time for recreation. One evening Mull, Latham, O'Rourke and Parker visited an Australian unit down the road a few miles. The Marines and the Commonwealth Division got on in famous style and whenever groups of them got together it was a signal for singing and jubilation.

The Australians had heard of Reckless and were interested in her behavior under fire. Before Latham and the others were through with the telling of it, their hosts were convinced the little horse had whipped the Chinese single footed. One of the Australians was so impressed he presented his hat to be given to Reckless. Anyone who has seen Australian troops will know their hats are distinctive and that such a present was of value.

It was a happy time. On the way home the Marines sang one of their favorite songs, to the tune of 'London Bridge Is Falling Down' —

Mushee, Mushee, eno nay
Eno nay, eno nay,

Mushee, Tnushee, eno nay
Ah so, desca.

There were other songs learned during the Korean war such as, 'When the Ice Is on the Rice' in Southern Honshu. And there was the new one they had just learned from the Australians —

Hark! Hark!
The herald angel sings
And Wally Simpson
Stole our King.

By the time the foursome arrived in camp it was late, but they awakened Reckless to show her the gift. By cutting holes on either side, it fit quite well. Reckless yawned her way through this tomfoolery and that made them laugh that much more.

Pat O'Rourke was not pleased with the hat on Reckless. "I don't like it, Joe," he told Latham. "I don't think it's dignified. A hat like that's something for the likes of that Army mule Francis to wear. He's a clown — Reckless ain't."

On more sober thought the others were inclined to agree. They decided that she would wear it only when she was in the immediate circle of the platoon. It was good for a laugh and with her close friends she would not be embarrassed. After a while, they went to bed.

From time to time Reckless was forced to wear the Australian hat, though she never did care for it. She agreed with O'Rourke that it was not dignified, besides, it tickled her ears. Something had to be done and she did it. Coleman left the hat hanging on a nail in the bunker. That settled the matter. The next morning all that could be found was the sweatband, a short piece of rim and half the crown. Fearful they might reblock it if she just tore it up, she had eaten enough to prevent any attempt of reclamation.

It was not so many nights later that Reckless was cause for a minor crisis among members of the platoon. It might have caused an internal rupture which could have affected the effectiveness of the unit.

It was a particularly cold night. A raw and bitter wind swept down from the Manchurian mountains and formed an ice sheeting on the Imjin River. It was much too cold to be out unless forced by the circumstance of having the watch or sentry post. Even the cheeriness of an evening with the Aussies was not enticement enough to face up to the jeep ride to get there. Units not facing the enemy, buttoned up early, turned the stove adjuster knob to 6 and settled down to a night at home camp.

Some wrote letters, some read and others computed the likely dates of rotation back to the United States. This latter was a pastime practiced by all, but enjoyed by none as the time to remain in Korea always seemed longer on paper than in the mental calculation. Latham and a few of his friends became involved in a poker game. Old hands at this military method of passing time and money, it proceeded with a minimum of talk. It was a cozy scene until Reckless stuck her nose into the overlap of the tent opening and proceeded to follow her nose inside. This created a stir as the wild wind swooped into the tent.

Latham sprang to close the canvas hole while Mull urged Reckless to a spot near the stove where she would not interfere with the game. Reckless let them know it was cold outside by a chilled blast from her hoarfrost-rimmed nostrils.

"I'm sorry, Reckless," Latham apologized for his seeming neglect, "I thought you were with Coleman and Carter."

He wiped the wind tears from her eyes, threw a blanket over her shoulders and turned the adjuster knob to 8. The potbellied stove sighed at a faster tempo.

"Let's go, Joe," Mull urged a return to the game as he dealt the cards.

Latham took his seat at the makeshift table. Mull, the dealer and game cashier, sat across from him. O'Rourke was on his right hand with S/Sgt. LaBarge on his left. Between LaBarge and Mull was T/Sgt. Parker. It was a sound, Marine-type poker game of dealer's choice between draw or stud with no wild cards.

The deal passed from man to man, poker chips clicked and clacked, cigarette smoke swirled and followed the heated stovepipe upwards into the peak and drained off slowly. The paunch of the stove glowed red, and without taking has eyes from the cards Latham turned the knob back to 6. Warm again, Reckless became interested in the game. She moved into a position directly behind Latham and peered over his shoulder. Engrossed in the game, the sergeant reacted to having someone standing behind him until he realized who it was.

"Whatta you think, Reckless, worth a bet?" He bet without awaiting an answer. All passed excepting Mull, who looked across the table and into the little mare's face as though seeking a hint from her. He called and lost.

The game went on with an interruption being caused when Reckless tried to eat a package of cigarettes at Latham's elbow.

"Hey, Reckless, knock it off." He retrieved a shredded package.

"Nicotine isn't good for horses," O'Rourke observed.

"Your bet," Parker told LaBarge.

Latham won three hands in a row and Reckless became engrossed in the growing stack of chips. She leaned over her friend's shoulder and took up a mouthful of blues.

"Hey!" Latham tried desperately to retrieve a portion of his wealth. The others laughed and laughed with little sympathy for the winner. Latham was able to salvage two whole chips and several pieces, but it was obvious Reckless had eaten several.

"Don't worry, Joe," Parker consoled, "those chips are made of plastic; they won't hurt her."

"I know that, but she must've eaten thirty bucks' worth."

"That's tough, Joe," Mull grinned. "I only pay off for whole chips."

The game broke up in argument as to how many blue chips Reckless had or had not eaten. She soon tired of the bickering and moved back to her place nearer the stove. O'Rourke summed up the whole thing as he crawled into his sleeping bag, "At least she goes first class, only eating the blue ones."

To this day, Latham figures Reckless owes him thirty dollars — maybe more.

Christmas came to Korea and Reckless never had such a ball in her life. There was candy, apples, carrots, cake, cola and an occasional beer, until she began to think hay was something to paw around and lie down on.

Doc Mitchell protested the rich fare.

"First thing you know," he warned Latham, "she'll be breaking out with hives or something."

"Christmas comes only once a year. She'll work it off as soon as we get back on the line."

CHAPTER IV

THIRTY DAYS IN RESERVE and the 5th Marines moved back into the line. Once again Reckless' regiment would face the enemy, but from a different sector. This time they would move to the east and relieve the 7th Regiment on the battle positions supporting the combat outposts East Berlin, Berlin, Vegas, Reno and Carson with smaller Ava farther to the west.

The 5th Marines were moving onto a battleground which would bring new glories to its colors, but would add many names to the final roll before it was done. And Reckless went to battle with her regiment and performed in a manner to earn the love and esteem of a corps of men to whom bravery is the rule rather than the exception.

For the little red horse the days of pampering were over. She carried pack load on pack load of equipment into the lines. There were small arms ammunition, grenades, rations, sleeping bags and communication wire to move forward. There was barbed wire for her own pasture.

Inasmuch as the 7th Marines had not had the foresight to enlist a horse, no accommodations, such as a pasture or horse bunker, could be expected. Whether nightfall found her forward or to the rear in the company CP area, she seemed content with whatever arrangements could be made for her comfort and safety. During the early phase of the exchange, if she were caught forward when darkness fell, she ate C rations and bedded down in the handiest position in defilade. While forward, if the incoming became heavy, the Marines in the immediate vicinity would shed flak jackets and cover her from head to tail. This meant, of course, that the donors went without the protection of the jackets.

The command frowned on such practice, but no orders were issued to put a stop to it. By this time the little horse was so firmly entrenched in the affections of the Marines that it is unlikely such an order would have been obeyed. To the rear, in the company CP area, an old dugout had been cleaned out and made available for occupancy. Here, too, the horse feed was brought forward from Changdan.

From the Imjin to the battle positions, the little horse met many Marines of her regiment she had not seen before. Heretofore she had worked mainly with the 1st Battalion. Now she was to live and fight with the 2d. And so she came to know the men of this unit as well as she did those of the 1st. As it turned out, the 2d was to become her favorite and the friends she made in this outfit were to have an important influence on the rest of her life.

Pedersen came to realize, sadly, that he was losing Reckless. She was no longer his, nor did she belong to the platoon. She had become a Marine, adopted by a regiment of Marines. In time, as she became known, she would be the pride of the Division — and the Corps. He knew that when he was transferred, as one day he must be, he could not take her with him. So as not to serve as a reminder of his wounds and long service with the platoon, he kept away from the regimental CP as much as possible.

Limping from wounds that were still unhealed, Pedersen established his command post not far from that of Fox Company of the 2d. A pasture was found in a valley that once had sheltered the farm hamlet of Panggi-dong. All that was left now of the once prosperous settlement were a few burned-out shells of huts. The air about them was heavy with the stench of old straw and living things that had only half burned in the fire that destroyed the village.

The main battle positions were four hundred meters to the north of the feeding grounds, but the pasture was masked from enemy observation and direct fire by a spur of Hill 120. This section of Korea was covered with tumbled-down, rocky hills without the stature to be called mountains. They were the foothills leading into the north-south spine of mountains that bisects Korea.

The pasture, bearing poor winter feed, was within easy mortar range of the Chinese who were in the habit of lobbing exploratory rounds into such pockets. Without aerial observation to correct or direct the fire, it was blind shooting. To guard against such danger, the platoon built an open-faced bunker, the opening to the friendly south, in which Reckless could take shelter if the incoming did become too severe.

The Ammunition Supply Point (ASP) from which Reckless would fill her pack with high explosive charges, was three hundred meters south and east of the pasture. As with all ammunition dumps, it was tucked away in defiladed position behind a sharp finger of an open canyon. The trail leading to the ASP from the pasture was an easy grade bordering what had once been a rice paddy. Two hundred meters of this, then a sharp swing to the left and the climb was made to cross the finger and drop sharply into the box canyon.

S/Sgt. John Lisenby established firing positions for his gun section on the ridge line fingers and spurs of Hill 120. These sites were east and north of the pasture and overlooked the MLR and from them the rifles could fire in direct support of East Berlin and Berlin, and into enemy held strong points known to Marines as Detroit and Frisco. (It is altogether possible the Chinese called them Canton and Shanghai.) Most important, though, was that Lisenby's weapons could reach out and fire into enemy held Hills 153 and 190, which faced on Outpost Vegas. When the battle was in doubt, this was to be of prime importance.

The route of Reckless from the pasture to the ASP has been described. The return to the firing sites involved the stiff, shoulder-hunching climb out of the canyon followed by the four-footed breaking on the descent onto the paddy trail, a right turn and the easy trail skirting the pasture. Two hundred yards east of feeding area there was a stiff, narrow, twisting trail rising at a 45 degree angle to the first ridge line of Hill 120. Reckless preferred to meet this obstacle with a racing start. With shell canisters threatening to jump from their rope moorings, she would charge the hill, Coleman having cast her free to make her own speed. She would just make the top in her final lunge and stand breathing heavily until her guide scrambled to her side. Usually she took off as she saw him nearing the top and made her way without guidance to one of the guns. The gun crew would see her coming and would call out to her. It was seldom that circumstances were so adverse or tense that someone didn't have a piece of hard candy for her. As far as she was concerned, the tinfoil wrapped hard candy was the best part of C rations. All the way back to the ASP she would suckle on it.

Sgt. Leon Dubois' 2d Section was assigned the area behind the MLR facing on outpost Carson in the sector of the 1st Battalion. Being nearly five thousand meters east from Reckless' pasture (longer by the lateral road net), it was impossible for her to service this weapon. S/Sgt. Harry Bolin's 3d Section was even farther away in the Ava outpost area, so that Lisenby and his section came to look upon Reckless as their own.

Naturally, Dubois and Bolin felt slighted and found pastures and dreamed up multiple reasons why Reckless should be assigned to them. Pedersen, however, was playing no favorites. Lisenby's gun positions could not be approached by vehicle, as could the others, and it would kill Marines to manpack the ammunition onto Hill 120.

The winter feed in the pasture was poor and, at the time, it was not feasible to make trips south of the Imjin to buy hay and grain from Korean fanners. Reckless was not doing well. The slim pickings in the pasture and C rations were not enough. Her barrel began to show signs of thin grass and no grain. Latham's paternal eye noted her condition at once. There was only one answer. He took the long trail to Lisenby's gun sites.

He said to the section leader, "Reckless is getting gaunt. I'll bet she's dropped fifty pounds. We've got to do something about it."

"We are—"

"What?"

"There's a section of Marines I know that are going to become grass pullers. On the side hills where it hasn't been trampled by tanks and trucks and Marines, there's still some pretty good grass. Each of us'll pull an armload a day until we get her some feed from across the Imjin."

"Okay. I'll get vitamin pills from Doc Mitchell and feed her those. They'll help."

Reckless did not take kindly to the pills. For the first time she looked with suspicion upon something to eat. Latham was firm, however, and was force feeding her the pills one by one when he noted that her tongue was swollen. He called Doc Mitchell into hurried conference. Mitchell prescribed terramycin. Within a week the swelling went down.

One day Colonel Lew Walt, new commander of the 5th Marines, was trooping the line in the Fox Company sector. On the slopes of Hill 120 he saw Marines on hands and knees pulling grass. After twenty-three years in the Corps, with a distinguished record of combat from Guadalcanal to Korea, he was intrigued.

"What are those men doing?" he asked.

"Pulling grass for Reckless. They haven't been able to get feed north of the Imjin and her pasture's pretty poor. Each man in the squad takes her some grass as he goes to chow at night."

Walt made a mental note that the next truck south of the river would return with feed for Reckless. He knew he had succeeded to a fine regiment, but he also knew he had inherited something special in this little red pony. He had seen her on the trails loaded with equipment while doing the work of ten men; he had been told of Marines shedding their flak jackets to cover her during heavy bombardments. This little horse was becoming as important to his men as the sight of another horse, Traveler, had been to the fighting men of the Army of Virginia.

Reckless did not suffer from lack of food for long. PFC Booker T. Crew, a recent arrival to the platoon, had occasion to drop by the regimental command post. He stopped in the galley to see an old friend. When he left he had a crate of Wheaties and several boxes of graham crackers. From then until the truck arrived from south of the river, Reckless ate hand-plucked grass, Wheaties, graham crackers, vitamin pills and the hard candy from C rations. Despite the long hours tramping the hills, she began to put on weight.

At this time the 1st and ad Battalions of the 5th Marines were in the line, with the 3d in reserve. Under the resolute leadership of Walt, a series of daylight raids were initiated against the enemy. The purposes of these raids were to check the "creeping" offensive of the CCF toward Marine main battle positions and to capture prisoners in order to improve the intelligence on enemy intentions.

In the spirit of an aggressive warrior, Walt presented his reasons for these raids: "Daylight operations offer several advantages over night raids. First and foremost, we can apply the full weight of our combined arms in support of the raiding infantry units. Good conditions of visibility will enable us to exploit our greatest advantage over the CCF — our Marine close air support means. Too, our artillery and mortars can employ observed fires, which will be highly effective against enemy units trying to reinforce cut-off comrades; daylight conditions will enable us to employ our gun and flame tanks with the maneuvering infantry in accordance with our tank-infantry doctrines. When we want to create conditions of limited visibility over portions of the battle area to inhibit the enemy's observations, we can use smoke — delivered according to plan by aircraft, artillery and mortars."

General Pollock agreed with the concept of his regimental commander and the plans were made and units went into rehearsal. Raid "TEX" was to be the first in the new year of 1953. It was designed to hit the enemy on Hill 139, which lay north of outpost Berlin and occupied an extension of the same hill mass. A reinforced rifle platoon led by Lt. Tom Bulger from Dog Company conducted the raid. It was a success and prisoners were taken. From Hill 120 Lisenby's gun section was in position to support the raid and for the first-time Reckless packed ammunition from dawn to dusk and was to hear the roar of many weapons.

Later the same month raid "CLAMBAKE" was designed against Unggoc. Remembering the run Reckless had taken with Baker in that area, many believed she should lead this strike against the Chinese. After all, she was the only Marine to have been so far forward of the line in this sector. Clambake, a company-sized raid, was led by Capt. Don Blanchard. Heavy fighting developed during the course of this strike and Bolin's gun section to the extreme right did outstanding work in providing covering fire for the withdrawing raiders.

In February, Capt. Dick Kurth's Fox Company struck a telling blow against the enemy on a raid known as "CHARLIE." The enemy strong point taken under assault lay on a hill mass called Detroit, which was directly north of Lisenby's gun positions. The range was less than six hundred yards. Kurth's raiders had to cross nearly three hundred yards of rice paddy before gaining the approaches to their objective. During this passage, which was covered by smoke, Lisenby's guns kept up an intense fire.

Reckless made twenty-four trips from the ASP to the firing sites during the course of the day while packing six rounds a trip. Pedersen estimated she traveled over twenty miles and her total carry was thirty-five hundred pounds.

It was dark before she returned to her pasture bunker. For the first time the Marines saw her with head hanging and no mischievous nuzzling for candy.

"She's really bushed," Coleman told Latham. "I didn't think she would make it onto the hill that last time. She had to make two runs at it, but she wouldn't quit."

Carter drove Pedersen alongside the bunker. From the back of the jeep he brought a bucket of warm bran mash. Reckless perked up. She sniffed the mixture and tasted it; she began to eat. While she finished her meal the Marines, two on a side, gave her a thorough rubdown — Native Dancer never received a better one. When they were through, Pedersen covered her with a blanket. She was asleep by the time they left.

All days were not so severe. There were many when there were no fire missions and Reckless hung to her pasture and fed and drowsed and became restive with the inactivity. General Pollock stopped by one day and, as always, inspected her feet. He found her shoes thin but in fair condition, but did not approve of the boots being worn by Coleman, which were run over at the heels and had seams that had pulled away from the sole.

He became a bit testy about this. His opinion was unaltered when it was explained that Coleman wore such a large boot it was virtually impossible to get a size to fit him; there wasn't a pair in the regimental supply big enough. The General told an accompanying staff officer, "I want Coleman to have a pair of boots of proper size by tomorrow."

"Yes, sir."

After the party left, Latham told Coleman, "If you don't get those boots, I'll take you to Seoul and have the Korean horseshoer fix you up at the same time he does Reckless."

"Don't worry," Pedersen advised. "Coleman'll have a pair of boots tomorrow."

Capt. Ted Mildner's company made "ITEM" raid against Ungoc (not the same as Unggoc!) in March as spring came slowly to Korea. The hillsides and paddies became green and spring flowers sprouted over the shell-torn land. Reckless thrived. The supply of rations from south of the river was stabilized and with the fresh green grass her coat took on a new, redder sheen as she lost her winter coat. There was little or no ammunition or supplies to carry at the moment and she worked off her energy by running impromptu races with her shadow. If there were an audience of any size, she would do the rocking horse act she had inherited from another Flame.

A replacement draft arrived from the United States and Reckless lost a number of friends. Gunnery Sergeant Mull journeyed to the pasture to say goodbye. Reckless appeared to be relieved when he told her Latham was taking his place. Sgt. Harry Bolin was to leave with Mull and his gun section was taken over by S/Sgt. Robert Reschke. Of immediate concern to Reckless, however, was the arrival of Sgt. Elmer Lively, who was assigned the second squad in Lisenby's section. They became firm friends in a short time and she discounted the fact that he once had been an Army man.

All was not entirely peaceful, however. Day by day the enemy were increasing their shelling of the regimental sector. Most of it fell on the outposts and main line, but more and more rounds expressed their hate in areas to the rear. One afternoon three mortar shells exploded in the pasture. Reckless' reaction was one of shock. She had learned enough of war to know that such goings on could be dangerous. She retired to her bunker.

Latham had seen the mortars explode and was running to get her to cover. As he told Pedersen later, "She knows what incoming is and she knows what the bunker's for. When those mortars exploded she didn't exactly run for cover, but she didn't let any grass grow under her feet either."

The next event that took place in Reckless' life can be attributed to boredom and lack of employment. One night, without explanation or reason, she left her pasturage and made her way forward to the main line. The Marines of Capt. "Big Dog" Young's "C" Company were delighted, though surprised, with their visitor. They made a great to-do over her and broke out all sorts of hoarded rations to give evidence of the warmth of their welcome.

To right and left along the line, the word was passed by field telephone, "Reckless is in the line."

"Whatta you mean?"

"Yeh, just walked in."

"What's she doing?"

"Eating C rations. From the way she's eating, that Reckless Rifle outfit don't feed her."

"Told them yet?"

"No, let 'em sweat."

When the enemy opened with a severe barrage of incoming, the Marine infantry were sorry they had not notified Pedersen. It was the heaviest bombardment to date. Front line rabbit holes and bunkers were too small for her, so she was rushed into a deeper section of trench. They did not know about her ability to kneel Volunteer flak jackets covered her from tail to ears. She didn't like the one over her head and shook it off.

"Keep your head down, Reckless. Are you crazy?"

"She must be to come up here when she doesn't have to."

On several occasions she was showered with dirt and pebbles by near misses. The humor of having her in the line quickly evaporated. Towards morning the bombardment subsided and Pedersen was notified to come and retrieve his friend.

It was generally supposed that Reckless had left home and sought the company of other Marines because she felt the RR Platoon was taking her pretty much for granted.

Combat Outpost Vegas lay twelve hundred meters in front of the main battle positions. Reno, to the north and west, was fifteen hundred meters from the MLR. The distance between the two was five hundred meters. Carson was eight hundred meters from the line and six hundred southwest of Reno. The three formed an obtuse triangle with Reno at the apex, and they came to be known as the Nevada Complex or the Iron Triangle, and the violent struggle to hold them, the "Battle of Cities."

These positions were named by Marine Lt. Colonel Tony Caputo whose battalion established and first occupied them. Caputo designated them after the Nevada gaming towns because, as he said, "It's a gamble if we can hold them."

This was a sound military observation inasmuch as the enemy line and strong points were on higher ground and looked down on all three. Carson was only four hundred meters from glowering Un-Gok; Reno was but three hundred meters from Hill 150, which was flanked by 153 to the east. Both of these enemy strongholds were backed up by the mighty Hill 190. Vegas also had 153 and 190 to contend with.

The numbers of these hills indicate their elevation and can be compared with Reno at 143 and Vegas a squatty 139. Despite the apparent hazard of occupying positions so near the enemy lines, the Marines were forced to it by the dictates of terrain. Reno, Vegas and Carson held the key to the city of Seoul. To lose these outposts meant the present line would become untenable. Further retraction southward was impossible without crossing the Imjin. If the Marines withdrew south of the river, the Army units on the right would be forced to fall back across the Samichon River and, once again, the gateway to the Korean capital would be open. With such a victory in view, the truce talks at Panmunjom would be delayed or broken off entirely.

It was known to the Marines that the Chinese could take any one or all three of these outposts if they were willing to pay the price. With most commanders, the cost would have been militarily unprofitable, but the ruthless Communist leaders ordered the assault. The battle for the Nevada Complex was joined and for a period of seventy-two hours reached a bloody crescendo seldom matched in warfare.

In the final days preceding the attack, however, the intentions of the enemy were not known. A prisoner captured earlier had informed the Marines that a heavy Chinese attack was to fall upon the 2 A. Army Division with a later assault on the Marine lines. This information could not be corroborated. To penetrate the fog of uncertainty and keep the enemy off balance, Walt devised the plan whereby the reserve battalion (the 2d) would place platoons on and around likely avenues of approach to ambush and capture prisoners. Another daylight raid on the enemy stronghold of Detroit was in rehearsal.

As Colonel Walt was to write later,

"The day of March 26, 1953, was normal during daylight working hours with no indication of what was to come except for a large amount of incoming, which had been occurring for several days previous. However, at precisely 1900 the enemy launched a coordinated attack by fire all along our regimental front. At the same time he attacked the center MLR regiment by fire and conducted limited diversionary attacks in platoon and squad strength against outposts Dagmar, Hedy and Esther in that sector. Also at 1900, there were several citings of enemy units moving in front of the Korean Marine Corps sector."

Shadings of night were growing swiftly as the enemy began his preparatory bombardment. Heavy mortar and artillery fire blanketed the MLR. The heaviest fire of all was on the three outposts. As night came on the sight of it was terrifying. The flashing eruptions ran the ridge lines and cascaded into the valleys and the sound of it was that of twenty tornadoes tearing at a countryside.

Throughout the night fighting of the heaviest, most violent sort developed in and around the Nevada Complex. By midnight the initial stage of the battle had gone to the enemy. Reno and Vegas were lost and the fate of the Marines manning the positions was unknown. Carson had held after being put to a severe strain. Reinforcing units sent along the Reno "rope" became heavily involved with superior enemy forces and were halted short of their objective. A similar setback met the unit dispatched to aid the Vegas garrison.

At 2:00 o'clock in the morning Walt was forced to a fateful decision. He requested permission to withdraw all troops to the rear of the MLR, to reorganize and launch a coordinated attack to retake Reno and Vegas during daylight. The remaining hours of darkness would be used to evacuate the wounded and dead.

Pollock granted Walt's request and the regimental commander called a meeting of his battalion commanders and staff in his COC bunker.

It was a grim gathering. Like most Marines these men had great belief in their abilities and a total faith in the courage and resolution of the Marine riflemen who would carry the fight to the enemy. It was simply a matter of giving the counterattacking force every assistance possible and completing the task with as few casualties as permitted.

CHAPTER V

WHEN THE ENEMY ATTACK by fire began, Latham braved the shelling and went to the pasture to check on Reckless. He found the little horse had taken refuge in the bunker. She was restive, nervous, and a fine sweat dampened her coat. She rubbed against Latham in obvious welcome as the terrifying crash and flash of exploding shells broke through her customary cairn. As it grew darker the night flares appeared to upset her more.

Latham tried to reassure her with little success. He was genuinely disturbed when she refused her night feeding of grain. He ran his hand along her damp neck.

"Don't get shook," he told her, "we've got a big day ahead of us." He left the grain in the feed box and returned to the platoon CP. Through the long hours of the night the men of the Reckless Rifles monitored by radio the battle of the outposts. Pedersen arrived from the regimental CP in the early morning hours.

He told his men, "The counterattack is set for 0930. Two-five will hit Vegas, Two-seven Reno. There is a shortage of smoke shells in the artillery. We have a good supply, so we'll be called on to help cover Two-five with smoke from Lisenby's guns. Until the jump off, we'll fire on targets of opportunity with HE."

It was still dark when Coleman made his way from the bunker to the pasture. A big-boned youth of great size and with the endurance of an ox, he led his charge from her shelter. The straps of the pack saddle were stiff with cold and it was awkward working in the darkness; his large hands fumbled with the cinch, breeching and breastplate straps.

Reckless was still nervous though the enemy incoming had fallen away to sporadic fire as the Chinese worked to consolidate positions gained during the night and save ammunition for the expected counterattack. Marine artillery and heavy mortars continued to fire on assembly areas and routes of approach the enemy would use to reinforce Reno and Vegas. As friendly shells sped overhead they filled the night air with a rasping whizzpp-whizzpp-whizzpp. Their final rasp would die for a moment to be followed by the crash of distant thunder. Then there was the occasional shell with a loose or imperfect rotating band, and that sounded like a thousand angry hornets.

The normal whizzpp fretted Reckless, but the unusual hornet-nest sound brought sweat to her flanks and neck. Coleman talked to her and tried to get her to eat a feeding of barley, but she would no more than nibble at it. She tossed her head and the breath came from her nostrils in a nervous snort. She tried to turn back into the bunker.

Coleman secured a small bag of grain to the pack along with rations for himself. He looked out over the darkened waves of land, the low scudding clouds overhead, and taking a shorter hold on the lead rope, moved a pace forward. Reckless hung momentarily and followed.

They left the pasture and took the trail to the Ammunition Supply Point. Once away from the flatlands of the paddy pasture they were walking through walls of shadows from the shallow hills nearby. They met Lively and his gun crew moving quietly in opposite direction.

Lively told Coleman, "Gunny Latham is waiting for you at the ASR. He'll help you load on the first few trips."

Lively went on into the darkness with his squad in file behind him. Coleman and Reckless continued westward. They climbed over the sharp finger and Coleman was beginning to sweat under his flak jacket. He slipped the rifle from his shoulder and slung it over the forward crosstree of the pack. They went on. In the darkness it was a tight scramble to the ridge that masked the supply point from the enemy.

On the top they paused for a breather and the wind from the northwest was fresh and whipping strong. Though friendly shells were still "whizzpering" above, Reckless no longer shook her head and pushed against him for comfort. Securing the lead rope to the pack, Coleman spoke to her and she led the way down the reverse slope. In the darkness the descent was steep and the trail uncertain. Coleman fell and a rock tore through his utility trousers and woolen underwear. His knee bled. Ahead of him he could hear Reckless slithering downward with all four feet breaking her progress. When he got to the bottom she was waiting with Latham.

Two ammunition trucks from the regimental dump had off-loaded and were grumbling over the rude trail that led to the main supply route a thousand yards away.

"Did she eat her grain?" Latham asked.

"Nope. Just nibbled at it. She didn't eat what you left her last night either."

"Leave her grain here. Try her after a while."

"Break out plenty of smoke," Latham directed the ammunition handlers. "We're the only ones who've got plenty of it. We'll start her out with eight rounds. See how she handles that load. Make each load six smoke and two HE."

The canisters were laced to the pack and Latham, with a slap of encouragement, turned Reckless to the first test. She took a deep breath, pricked her ears sharply forward and charged the hill. As Latham and Coleman scrambled upwards behind her they were met with a small avalanche of rocks and dirt she had kicked loose.

Breathing heavily, they gained the ridge line. Reckless saw them coming and started down the far side. They had to press their pace to keep up with her. It was easier for all on the trail skirting the paddy before the sweat-letting surge over the finger. Off the finger, the two Marines thought she might turn into the pasture, but she kept to the trail.

The first light of dawn was lightening the sky behind Hill 120 as Reckless came to the approaches leading to it. She knew what faced her and without a word of urging broke into a trot and then a gallop. The ammunition canisters bounced and banged and Latham was fearful the bindings would break. With a load of nearly two hundred pounds she gained speed slowly, but hit the sharp rise at a run. The incline was a forty-five-degree angle with two hundred fifty feet of turning, twisting trail before the first restful spur was reached. Her flanks were still heaving and there was a rim of lather under the breeching when Latham gained her side.

Lisenby had established various firing sites on the slopes of the hill mass of 120. Directly below was the MLR. In front of the line was a four-hundred-yard strip of mined paddy land and then the hills of the enemy. Because of the curvature of the line, which at this point ran in a northeasterly direction, Vegas and Reno were southeast of the gun positions. The gun crews could see in front of the outposts and could fire into the flanks of the enemy on Hills 190, 150 and 153.

It was still wanting a half hour to sunrise, but Vegas and Reno and the enemy-held hills were coming clear in the growing light. Marine artillery and heavy mortars were mushrooming the ridge lines with black HE and white phosphorous, called "Willie Peter" by the troops. On Vegas there was no sign of life, friendly or enemy. The only sign of war or that men had fought and died on this hill a few hours before were the hollow-eyed holes left by shells and mortars, the jagged, caved-in trench line and tactical wire ground to a thorny pulp.

Pedersen roved the high ground searching through binoculars for targets as he directed the shooting. He was paying special attention to the approaches to Vegas from the north. Anything to kill, maim, harass and delay the enemy until the counterattack could jump off. No smoke shells, however, would be used until orders were given to cover the advancing Marines.

Behind the lines tanks growled into ridge-line tank wallows scooped out by bulldozers and, hull down, began to fire. Dubois and his section opened up in the Carson sector as did Reschke from behind Ava. High angling over all were the 4.2 (four deuces) mortars and behind all these were the batteries of artillery, medium and large, beginning to increase the tempo of fire.

Then came the sound that always made the most blasé veteran cock an ear. It was the frenzied tearing of air currents by a rocket ripple. One hundred forty-four rockets passed overhead in nearly solid flight. At the sound of them Marines all along the line looked northward. On the forward slopes of Hill 190 there was the clustered twinkle of dozens and dozens of orange lights and then the lights were lost in the Bikini blossom of yellow smoke and dust. Long seconds later came the roar of thunder. Even with that the Marines did not turn away, but waited for the second, smaller flight.

"Ah! The alibi round," meaning those rockets that had lain stillborn in their tubes on the initial firing had been rejuvenated and sent on their way of destruction. It was one sound of war that Reckless never understood or became accustomed to hearing.

At the beginning of the day the recoilless rifles had a small supply of shells in the vicinity of each firing position. Reckless began the day working against this backlog. Her efforts were augmented by members of the squad who were packing three rounds a trip. As the day wore on, time and terrain began to take their toll of Marine-packers and the little horse was making two trips for each of her friends.

The gun crews were following the established tactic of firing five rounds and shifting to an alternate site. The most distant position from the supply point was seven hundred yards, the nearest five hundred fifty. Despite the ruggedness of the terrain, Reckless was making the long haul in twenty minutes and the shorter one in twelve. During the early phase there was little or no counterfire from the Chinese. They were intent on waiting out the blistering Marine fire and saving ammunition for the infantry attack they knew they must face.

At daybreak weather reports indicated the wind would be blowing at nine to eleven knots in a southerly direction. Under these conditions it would be most difficult to maintain an effective screen over the advancing Marines. Because of the shortage of smoke ammunition it would be impossible to cover units attacking both Reno and Vegas. Pollock gave Walt permission to withhold the assault on Reno to allow maximum preparation on Vegas.

As the hour for the counterattack approached, every weapon at the command of the Marines was turned to the task of supporting the infantry. Smoke shells began to blossom and drift down wind. Lisenby's gun crews began pumping two smoke shells a minute onto the slopes ahead of the advancing infantry. A gray fog grew and drifted southward. In the draws the smoke held well and provided cover, but in the open the wind caught it up and dispersed it.

The enemy, aware the attack was forming, began a heavy counterfire. Pedersen roamed the hillside with his binoculars, seeking enemy gun and mortar positions. When such a site was discovered, he would direct Lively or Ober to take it under fire. Except for the tanks, the recoilless rifles were the only weapons where the gunners could see the target, whereas the artillery and heavy mortars were dependent on forward observers. Because of this Pedersen's guns could fire on targets directly in front of friendly troops.

Targets were plentiful and with the constant planting of smoke shells the backlog of ammunition dwindled until the gun crews were loading directly from Reckless' pack. Latham increased her load to eight rounds and watched with concern as she climbed the steep hillside.

Better to support the thin line of attacking Marines, Pedersen moved the gun sites forward until the guns were firing over the main line itself. From this position the guns could bring enfilade fire onto the enemy on Vegas and flanking fire on reinforcements attempting to move down from Hill 190. This meant a longer haul for Reckless and her fellow Marine ammunition carriers, and it also meant they could be brought under direct fire from the enemy on Detroit and Frisco.

Shortly after midday, Pedersen spotted several hundred Chinese reinforcements moving from Hill 139 to Vegas. He reported his find to battalion and turned Lively's attention to this lucrative target. From the exposed-gun position the enemy could be seen running from defiladed positions across a two-hundred-yard strip of paddy land to shelter behind a finger of Vegas itself. This force was taken under fire by the heavy mortars, artillery and aircraft with Lively and Ober throwing round after round of HE and WP into the running Chinese.

Enemy counterfire shifted to the telltale smoke and dust blown up by the weapons. Incoming rose from sporadic to heavy, but Pedersen knew a shift in positions would cost time. The rifles stayed where they were set in with Lively and Ober firing as rapidly as possible. The gun barrels grew hot.

Reckless came off the paddy floor with her twenty-first load of the day. She was wet with sweat and white rims of lather curled over the breeching and breastplate straps. She made her run at the sharp spur. Each time it appeared as though she would not make it, yet each time she did. On the top she paused with flanks heaving. Though she was obviously very weary, her rest period was never for long before she turned toward the sound of the guns. They were her bellwether.

The incoming was heavy as the enemy tried to destroy the weapon firing directly into the ranks of their reinforcing unit. The roar and blast shook the ground as rocks, shrapnel and dust filled the air. Reckless made her way along a spur, across a shallow draw and onto the nose. They unloaded her in the partial shelter of an old, bashed-in bunker. A cluster of three enemy mortar shells roared in and burst. The burning, searing white phosphorous vomited in all directions. The Marines dived for cover for there is nothing quite so feared by fighting men as the molten fury of phosphorous. Reckless recoiled from the sizzling white cloud. For a moment it appeared that terror might make her bolt.

"Easy, girl!" Latham whipped off his flak jacket and put it over her head. The semidarkness eased her panic. His hand along her neck wiped away more of her fear.

"Okay, let's go." He gave her a hearty slap and removed the jacket. She turned out of the shallow hole and took the trail back to the supply point. The guns ceased fire and shifted positions. Few, if any, of the enemy reinforcements reached Vegas.

Latham followed and once they were behind the protection of the masking canyon arm, he removed the pack saddle and watered and fed her. While she ate he rubbed her thoroughly, paying particular attention to her feet and legs. He gave her another half hour rest following the meal. When the pack was replaced and the ammunition canisters roped in place she took the trail back without urging.

Throughout the long day of fighting Reckless continued to carry her pack loads of ammunition through the corridors of blasting mortar and artillery shells. Sometimes she made the trip with Coleman and other Marines, at other times she went alone. On one trip a piece of shrapnel flicked over the left eye and blood ran into the white of her blaze. Pedersen wiped it clear and patted it dry with iodine. Later in the day she was cut again on the left flank, but neither wound appeared to unsettle her. She had become an automaton. Fatigue had taken its toll and drained her free of nerves, but as long as they would load and unload her, she kept to her task. No longer did she run at the hill rising sharply from the paddy — rather she crept up the twisting trail and paused to take two or three rest periods en route.

Though water was in short supply, Latham drained bottles into his helmet and saw to it that she replaced the moisture she was losing by sweating. He also lightened her load to six rounds and gave her a twenty-minute rest and grain in the late afternoon. From his combat rations he gave her squares of chocolate as an energy restorer.

Lisenby's section continued to pour shells into enemy positions. From their gun positions the Reckless Riflemen could watch the Marine assault forming; they could see the lines melt away and the attack stall, and they redoubled their efforts to assist their fellow Marines. Lively's gun barrel grew hot. It came to white heat and crystallized. The gun went out of action about the time it grew too dark for further shooting.

During the day Reckless made fifty-one trips from the ASP to various gun positions. She carried three hundred eighty-six rounds — more than nine thousand pounds of explosives. Pedersen estimated the distance she traveled to exceed thirty-five miles.

She stumbled and her head hung low as she came off the hill for the last time in the cool darkness. She walked in a file with the section and the Marines talked to her and told her what a great little horse she was. A few meters across the line the battle still raged and a jigsaw pattern of tracer bullets laced the darkness. Overhead friendly shells still whispered their way to enemy positions and rocket ripples still painted the ridge lines an orange red. Enemy incoming blasted and rocked the lines and hills to harass and halt the Marines from reinforcing Estes on the slope of Vegas and resupplying Ingalls on Carson.

Reckless paid scant heed to this roar of battle as she appeared to sleep-walk the trail with her friends. Her pace quickened a bit when they turned off the trail and into the pasture. In front of the open-faced bunker she let out a great sigh as Latham removed the pack saddle. Carter brought a can of water in the jeep. While she ate a generous helping of grain, Latham and Coleman rubbed her down. When she was through with the grain, Latham let her drink again and then piled fresh straw deep on the bunker floor. It took considerable coaxing, but he got her to lie down as he had taught her at Changdan. He left her covered with a blanket.

When Latham arrived at the CP he reported to Pedersen that all was well with Reckless. In turn Pedersen told Latham, "Orders have come through relieving me of the platoon. Lt. Bill Riley's taking my place in the morning."

Once again Latham was faced with a dual loss. "Where are you going, Lieutenant?"

Pedersen smiled, "Not too far, Joe. I'm taking command of the company. I won't be far away."

"Then Reckless can stay with me?"

"Of course. You'll need her tomorrow. I've got a new rifle coming up tonight. Have Lively check it over and be in position to start firing at first light."

"Yes, sir."

During the day the Marine infantry had experienced fighting of the heaviest sort. Despite the most gallant efforts by Dog and Easy companies of the Second Battalion, little ground was gained. Late in the afternoon Fox of Seventh Marines carried on the attack and gained the lower trenches of Little Vegas. A prisoner was captured. He proved to be a willing talker and an intelligent soldier. He informed Walt and the staff that they were being opposed by the 358th Regiment of the 40th Communist Chinese Army. He was proud of his unit and boasted it was the best in the army and the honor of leading the assault on Reno and Vegas had gone to the 358th because it was the best. When the Marine counterattack on Vegas began they had been told, "You will hold to the last man. Those who withdraw will be sent back." He said casualties had been heavy and another regiment was being sent forward.

During the night a supply train got through to Carson which assured the successful defense of this outpost. Plans were laid for the continuation of the attack on Vegas and the neutralization by fire of Reno. Now that it was known the Marines had been removed, the heaviest weapons would be turned on both objectives.

Pedersen turned over to Riley and went to the pasture to see Reckless before reporting in to the Antitank Company CP. Before daylight Lisenby's section was moving along the trail toward their gun positions. Coleman found Reckless gaunt and hungry. It could be seen that the day before had melted many pounds from her small frame. While she dug into an oversized meal of barley, Coleman rubbed her down. She accepted the pack without protest, but when they struck off toward the ASP Coleman noticed she was stiff-gaited.

Latham waited for them at the ASP and examined her legs and feet with care. Coleman told him about her obvious soreness.

"She's gimpy from overwork, Coleman. She should work out of it when she gets warmed up."

Latham's prognosis was correct. By the end of the first trip she moved along freely. Her battle attitude was altogether different on this second day as well. The day before seemed to have given her a fatalistic approach to her life with Marines. No longer did she become skittish over unusual noises and now her sweating was normal because of hill climbing and not excessive from worry.

As Lively was to report, "A round of Willie Peter landed about thirty yards from her and she didn't even look around at it."

It was well she had become accustomed to war for this second day of the battle for Vegas was to bring a cannonading and bombing seldom experienced in warfare. In denying Reno to the enemy by fire the heaviest shells and one thousand pound bombs completely erased the crest. Later in the morning twenty-eight tons of bombs and hundreds of the largest shells turned the crest of Vegas into a smoking, death-pocked rubble. Reckless shivered under the shock of the concussion, but it was a muscular reaction rather than from nerves.

Easy Company of the 5th Marines came back to the battle and in a valiant sweep upwards gained the hill. The Reckless Rifles aided materially in this final drive by firing directly into the trenches ahead of the attacking infantry. Another night and day of heavy fighting repulsed counterattack after counterattack until the Chinese command had expended two regiments. Even they could not afford to pay a higher price.

The Battle of Vegas was over and within a short time the Marines were relieved by the Turkish Brigade. For the first time in many months the 1st Marine Division was to leave the line for a rest.

Riding in the trailer Gentleman had loaned them six months before, Reckless and her regiment moved across the Imjin River to Camp Casey. It was near the village of Tongduchon-ni on the Sinch'on River and fifteen miles, as a helicopter flies, from the battle line. Only in the quiet of the night could the big guns be heard. It was a beautiful farming section and the grass was tall and green and the hillsides bright with flowers. At first sight Reckless liked the area and the location of her camp, which was just down the road and around a bend from the Second Battalion. All the Marines she knew well told her they would have a lot of fun. She did.

CHAPTER VI

SHORTLY AFTER ARRIVAL in Camp Casey, Pedersen received transfer orders. As soon as he learned the sad news he called Latham to his tent.

"Joe, I've got my orders. There's nothing I can do about it this time."

"I'm sorry to hear it, Lieutenant. What about Reckless? I'd like to take up a collection and pay you back."

"Only in part, Joe. I always want to keep a monetary interest in her. We've got to think about getting her back to the States. We can't leave her out here when the division goes home."

"I've been thinking of that, too. The CO of the Second Battalion is interested in her. He said he'd get her home."

"General Pollock will do all he can. I know that. Anyway, well have to wait until this war is over."

"She may be an old mare by that time."

Latham called the platoon together and in a matter of minutes had enough money to repay the officer. Riley joined Pedersen when he went to say goodbye to the little horse. She was feeding on lush spring grass and came to meet them. Pedersen ran his hand along her sleek neck.

"Take good care of her, Bill."

"Don't worry, Eric. She'll be okay."

Captain James Schoen assumed command of the company and Pedersen departed for his new duty station.

Reckless found herself to be somewhat of a celebrity. A constant flow of visitors came to the camp to see her and she was interviewed by several newsmen. Her picture and an article about her appeared in the Tokyo edition of the *Stars and Stripes* and the commanding officer of the Second Battalion said he would write about her for the *Saturday Evening Post*. General Pollock dropped by to see that she was happy and wherever she went Marines called greetings to her. With rest, green grass and grain she soon regained the spirit of Changdan and put on boisterous exhibitions of running and jumping. She took delight in taunting Latham by making believe she would run him down. There were several near collisions as she narrowed the distance of her misses.

"Someday," Riley warned, "she's going to make a mistake and we'll be looking for a new gunnery sergeant."

Within a matter of days the regiment was in a turmoil of moving again. They were hardly settled in Camp Casey before they took off on an amphibious exercise. The question was raised, "Is Reckless going?" The answer was unanimous, "Of course, she's going! Put her on the loading list. She will ride in the LST with the tanks."

And that is how Reckless came to be the first horse in history to go on an amphibious landing with the Marines. The loading lists were made up and submitted to the Navy. The regiment was to move from Camp Casey to Inchon, fifty-five miles, by train. Because the trains in Korea run on an indifferent schedule, such a trip could take anywhere from six to twelve hours. Schoen decided his unit could go by train and that he and Coleman would transport Reckless to the seaport town by trailer, Latham was to stay in camp with the rear echelon. He promised to have a shoemaker located by the time they were back.

After seeing the company aboard the train, Schoen and Coleman, accompanied by PFC Eagle Trader, began the journey to Inchon. They spent the night at the Marine supply base at Ascom City and arrived at Inchon early the following morning.

A replacement draft of Army troops, freshly arrived from the United States, were debarking from a ship when Reckless and her retinue arrived on the dock. PFC Eagle Trader jumped out, dropped the tail gate and without fuss Reckless scrambled to the ground.

At this performance the soldiers went bug-eyed.

"Hey! Lookit! The Marines've got a horse. Horse Marines, seagoing horse Marines. They're taking her on that boat!"

None of the Marines present made any attempt to enlighten the "Doggies." Anyone who had been in Korea more than ten minutes should have recognized her on sight.

The next hurdle to Reckless' sea venture came from the Navy. The Navy can hardly be blamed, for they did not know they were dealing with a Marine heroine. The best account of her appearance on the ramp to go aboard the LST came from Lt. Col. Ed Wheeler, who commanded the 1st Battalion at the time Pedersen was wounded for the third time. Wheeler was now executive officer of the Regiment.

Wheeler wrote:

"I recall that as Reckless and her party approached the LST they were halted by a loud hail from the bow. The hailer proved to be the Navy skipper. He was considerably exercised over the proposition of transporting livestock in his clean tank deck. It was obvious his embarrassment was profound when the Marines pulled out a loading plan approved by him, which included in its myriad columns and figures, '1 horse, w/appurtenances.' From that point on, I imagine that this officer is a firm believer in reading 'the small print' in any loading list he signs."

Reckless gained admission to the ship and Coleman made a stall for her between tanks. Two days' rations were unloaded from the trailer and she was ready for her first sea voyage. The bulk of her feed was in a truck on another ship and she would marry up with it on the beach.

The plan for the exercise was to have the regiment and supporting troops land on a beach several hundred miles south of Inchon. After landing and penetrating in a mock war for several thousand yards, they would withdraw, board ship and return to Inchon and Camp Casey. This would be the first amphibious landing for the regiment since scaling the seawall of Inchon in 1950 under battle conditions.

Reckless would land with the tanks and go about her task of transporting ammunition inland for the Reckless Rifles.

Soon after sailing the task force came into heavy weather. The excitement of the trip, combined with the smell of gasoline from the tanks and the roll of the vessel, made Reckless sick. Coleman and Eagle Trader did what they could for her and wished desperately that "Doc" Mitchell were along to prescribe for her. They were rebuffed by the ship's corpsman when they asked for seasick pills. He thought they were crazy. The tank deck had become messy and the Navy personnel were unhappy with its condition.

Captain John Kaufman, U. S. Navy, commodore of the LST squadron, flew his "flag" from the same ship in which Reckless was riding. He had heard of her presence on board and had gone below decks to visit her. When he heard of her seasickness he saw an excellent opportunity to taunt his Marine friends Wheeler and Colonel Harvey "Joe" Tschirgi, who was now commanding the Fifth.

The storm forced a change in plan for the exercise and a conference was called in the task force flagship. Kaufman's display of anger was convincing. He waited until all concerned were seated and then asked in a loud voice, "When're you Marines going to get that haybag off my ship?"

Army observers on the operations were startled to learn there was a horse in the Marine complement.

Tschirgi asked, "How's she doing, Jack?"

"How's she doing? Brother! You should see. That tank deck will never be the same again."

Tschirgi grinned, "You may have to put up with her longer than you expected. We're only going to land the infantry — the tanks, artillery and Reckless will stay aboard."

There was less acting in Kaufman's reaction to this news. "My ship has won the 'E' for being the cleanest vessel in the fleet two years hand running, but I can assure you Reckless is going to end that tenure."

The heavy seas continued and only the infantry went ashore. Two days later they re-embarked and the task force headed for Inchon. By now Reckless had overcome her "allergy" and she was voracious. In no time at all she was finished with the scant rations that had come aboard with her. Coleman and Eagle Trader were able to arrange for cabbage and oatmeal from the ship's galley, but the cabbage caused another stomach upset. The crew groaned and Coleman worried over her obvious loss in weight. How could he explain to Latham?

Kaufman sent a dispatch to Tschirgi: "Reckless out of rations. We may have to eat her before she eats us."

A small boat transfer of hay and barley was effected by Cpl. Howard Richie and the rest of the trip was uneventful. When she debarked there was a noticeable lack of a return invitation from the Navy.

In the absence of the main body, the rear echelon turned to with a will and Camp Casey was a welcome sight — with screened mess halls, tents in which each man had a cot, and daily access to the PX. Recreational equipment was distributed and athletic fields leveled so the Marines turned to games, Latham had a surprise for Reckless when he introduced her to Jimmy Lee. Jimmy was an orphan Latham had come across and took in to live with him. The three were inseparable from then on. Coleman was relieved of caring for her while Latham and Jimmy took over the job.

This was the first time Reckless had been with the Marines when they were completely relaxed and on a half-day training schedule. The rest of the time was spent at games or around the slop chute.

One day she posed for a picture with Riley, Latham and Lively's squad. Doc Mitchell was there, too. The purpose of the picture was to record a challenge to Native Dancer to race in *The Paddy Derby*. A letter was drafted to Alfred Vanderbilt submitting the terms of the race to be held at Upsan Downs: A side bet of $25,000 (each man in the 1st Marine Division to put up $1.00) over a distance of one mile and a half of hills and rice paddy; weight to be carried, eight rounds of 75mm. ammunition (192 pounds). There would be no riders. Both horses would be turned loose and the first to reach the firing Reckless Rifle would be judged the winner.

A few days later Native Dancer was defeated in the Kentucky Derby. Doubtlessly this loss discouraged Mr. Vanderbilt for the platoon never received an answer to their proposal. Most of the Marines were convinced she would have won in a walk.

A regimental parade was held to honor and decorate the heroes of the Battle for Vegas, and the division band made the hills echo with martial music. To Reckless this was more exciting than being under fire. The band music made her skin ripple and when it came time for the platoon to come into line and pass in review, she wanted to do her rocking horse gait, but Coleman wouldn't let her.

One day General Pollock came by for the last time before returning to the United States. As usual, he gave her a thorough inspection. He was as upset over the condition of her shoes as he had been over Coleman's months before. Riley assured him that Latham was taking her to the Seoul race track the next day in an effort to find a cobbler she would allow to touch her feet.

Though the change in command of the division cost Reckless a friend, she gained another in Major General Ran McC. Pate. Once he met her the new commander never passed her camp without dropping in for a chat.

The following day, Latham and Jimmy Lee drove Reckless to Seoul. The Gunnery Sergeant, who knew the little horse better than any Marine, was impressed by her apparent excitement as the trailer came to a stop by the track stables. He knew Pedersen had bought her at the track, but knew nothing of her previous owner. It was obvious by the number of Koreans who circled his vehicle that she was remembered by all of them. Jimmy had not learned enough English as yet to be of much help, but Latham made his wants known by lifting a hoof and pointing at her shoe.

A Korean with an arm missing stepped from the throng and Reckless greeted him eagerly. He smiled at Latham.

"My name Choi."

"Hello, Joe. My horse needs new shoes."

Choi slipped his arm over Reckless' neck. "We fix." He shouted in Korean and a youngster scurried away and disappeared behind the stables. Choi said to Latham, "I know Ah-Chim-Hai long time." He held his hand out to indicate her size as a weanling.

"What did you call her?" Latham asked.

"Ah-Chim-Hai. What you call her?"

"Reckless."

Choi repeated the word with a frown. He shook his head, it meant nothing to him. Taking the lead rope from Latham he led Reckless into an end stall. She appeared to be in familiar surroundings.

A young Korean came around the end of the stable. He was breathing heavily from running. Without speaking, he went into the stall and Latham saw Reckless nuzzle against him.

Knowing she was in safe hands, Latham took Jimmy in search of the mess galley of the Army helicopter unit. After coffee and doughnuts with the Army, they returned to the stable. Reckless had been expertly shod and was ready. Choi was there too, but the horseshoer was gone. Latham asked for him, but all he could get from Choi was a shrug. With the trailer backed against a bank, Reckless clambered in. Latham pressed a handful of hwan into the hand of the Korean and drove away.

With little warning the Marines were ordered back into the lines. The move was made in the midst of heavy summer rams and Reckless found herself once again in Changdan. The Second Battalion was occupying the line supporting the outposts Hedy to COP 2. It was a complete cycle for the RR Platoon and the little mare.

The same conditions prevailed around COP 2 as had existed to bring Reckless into the Corps. While the truce talks went on the tenacious, patient Chinese continued to dig. Considerable headway had been made inasmuch as the troops occupying the sector while the Marines were in reserve would not risk a stray shot in the circle to hinder the "great ditch of China" excavation.

The Second Battalion had been in occupancy of the sector but a short time when Riley was called to the COC bunker.

The commanding officer told him, "Luke is going to dig us out of COP 2 if we don't do something to stop him. Jagoda tried walking his sixties onto them, but one round got away and landed in the circle. I'm still bleeding from the chewing out I got. I want you to take one of your rifles out here."

He pointed to the confluence of the corridor and the circle. "Give them a good pasting. Just be careful not to fire into the Holy Land."

Riley grinned. "Yes, sir!" He practically ran from the bunker to get on with the job. Every day thereafter Riley moved a gun onto the molar and took the enemy under heavy fire. There was a noticeable lack of digging enthusiasm by the Chinese after Riley and his guns took over.

The war continued with Reckless and her platoon roving the line from COP 2 eastward to Ava. The 3rd Battalion saw heavy action in the Hedy-Bunker sector and Reckless came under fire again on the same hillside where she first experienced the blast of incoming. Farther to the east the 1st and 7th Marines came to grips with the enemy in the Vegas sector. For reasons the Marines could never understand, the Turks had been ordered to evacuate Vegas and without it the Marines were hard pressed to hold the line. It was a costly battle.

Then the truce was signed. The Second Battalion side slipped to the south where it took up new positions from the Panmunjom corridor to the Imjin River. Reckless and her platoon moved with the Second and made a comfortable camp in a shallow-hilled valley not far from an abandoned ferry crossing site. The approach to the river at this point was gentle and the shore was black sand. Reckless spent her days in the hills stringing communication wire to new positions. It was an easy life for the most part and she put on weight.

During this period the commanding officer of the Second would invite Reckless, Riley and Latham to his bunker overlooking the Imjin to sit out the cool of the evening and talk about her. With notebook in hand, the older officer wrote page after page as Latham and Riley talked. It was at one of these meetings plans were discussed about her trip to the States.

Latham told the officer, "I know it sounds crazy, Colonel, but I want to take Reckless and Jimmy home with me."

"How many children do you have, Gunny?"

"Two girls. The younger was only two months old when I shipped out for Korea."

"What would your wife say?"

"She's all for it. We like kids, horses and dogs."

"Getting Jimmy home poses more of a problem than Reckless. This I'll promise you, Joe, I'll get Reckless home."

"That's going to make a lot of Marines happy," Riley said.

"If I can't take Jimmy, I'll fix him up with some good family and see that he's sent to school."

"Okay. You take care of Jimmy and I'll see to Reckless. My dad was a great horseman. I've been around horses all my life, but I've never known one like Reckless. Obviously, she had fine treatment and excellent training before Pedersen bought her."

"I don't know who he bought her from, but the Koreans at the track should know. One guy told me her Korean name, but I can't remember it."

"I'm being transferred to the Kimpo regiment. Over there I'll have time to get into Seoul. I'll try to track down her story."

"I'm sorry you're leaving, Colonel."

"I am too, Bill. I yelled so loud they could hear me way back in division without the telephone, but it didn't do any good. Tomorrow night is my sayonara. Bring Reckless and we'll make the rounds of the various units. We'll start out at staff NCO's tent. Better bring the trailer to get her to Easy and Fox companies."

"Yes, sir."

As Riley and Latham and Reckless walked along the narrow pathway toward the jeep park, the officer called out, "Bill, I've arranged for your transfer into the battalion. You'll be assigned to Fox Company."

"Thank you, Colonel."

For a long while after they left the battalion commander sat and watched the night shadows grow on the river and the traffic lights move across Freedom Bridge. After a time he had to light the Coleman lantern to see his notes.

The next evening the four of them journeyed about the battalion area saying farewell. As she had done from the first, Reckless joined in and no matter how crowded a tent or bunker became it never fretted her. Her nonchalant acceptance of being with Marines led Riley to say, "You know, Colonel, Reckless has forgotten she's a horse."

All hands had fun and there were laughter and singing. Major Tom Fields joined the group as they went from unit to unit. It was late when they returned to the battalion CP and raided the officers' galley. While the others had Spam sandwiches, Reckless drank a tin of coffee and ate bread covered with peanut butter. They all had a tear-rolling laugh when the peanut butter clung to the roof of her mouth. A second tin of coffee helped, but she still made faces as her tongue rolled the stuff off her palate.

The next morning the battalion commander and Reckless paid a visit to Lt. Jack Leversee, unit surgeon, where a remedy was sought for the residual inertia that had been built up the night before.

In October Latham received orders to return to the United States, as did Coleman. Along with them Reckless would lose other friends like Kelly, Cassitty and her unwilling rider into the mine field, Baker. Latham arranged for Jimmy to live with a family nearby where he could see Reckless often and the members of the platoon promised to care for him. Latham had no worry over lack of attention for Reckless. Should the unit become careless they would soon be brought to account by General Pate who never failed to visit her and inspect her bunker whenever he was in the Second Battalion sector.

Lt. William McManus, who had relieved Riley, expressed it well, "The surest way I know of getting locked up is to have the General find her bunker dirty and Reckless unhappy."

High excitement was generated during the charity fund drive for Navy Relief. One night members of the Four Point Two Mortar (Four Deuces) unit spirited Reckless from her bunker and hid her in another near their camp. The plot had been engineered by the division special service officer. The morning after her disappearance it was announced that Reckless had been kidnaped and was being held for ransom. Tickets were distributed for purchase. They read, "FIRST MARINE DIVISION MARINE CORPS MEMORIAL ASSOCIATION. RANSOM RECKLESS." The tickets cost one dollar.

To the RR Platoon there was little humor in the situation. They were assured she was safe, but had no confidence in the ability of the abductors to care for her properly. How could outsiders possibly know her feeding habits? On cold nights would they take her into a stove-heated tent? Headed by Sgt. Lively, the platoon donated four hundred dollars to the Ransome Reckless Fund. The division poured in over twenty-eight thousand dollars and Reckless was returned. She appeared to have enjoyed her stay with the Four Deuces.

Master Sgt. John Strange, now the senior NCO in the AT Company, felt Reckless had been neglected and had gone too long without receiving official and public recognition of her services. Captain Andrew Kovach agreed. She should be promoted to sergeant and her acts of courage read aloud during a company formation. First, though, she must have a distinctive uniform. Kovach designed a blanket and turned it over to the platoon for comment and criticism. After a few minor changes, Lt. Herbert Loui drove into Seoul where he found a Korean tailor who would do the job.

The parade blanket was to be of red silk trimmed in gold. There was to be a Globe and Anchor on either side and the proper unit identification. The blanket would cost fifty-one dollars. Another collection was taken.

A week later the uniform was ready and Reckless appeared to be impressed when she had her first fitting. All hands agreed it was a first-rate job though PFC Billy Jones was heard to remark that the American eagle atop the globe "looks like a tired Korean sparrow."

She had not modeled the blanket more than a few minutes when the silk stirred her interest and she nibbled at the front edge. Lively was quick to notice this and remembered the tales of her eating the Australian hat and Latham's poker chips.

He cautioned, "Never leave her alone with that blanket. She'll eat it like she did that hat and we can't be putting out fifty bucks every few weeks."

It took Reckless nine months to make a prophet of Lively, but she came through in winning style. She proved an old proverb, "A good horse does everything well."

All was now in readiness for the ceremony. Kovach so informed Col. Elby Martin, then commanding the 5th Marines. Would he and the General come to the AT area to present Reckless with sergeant's stripes? Of course! Martin arranged a date with the General and the unit began a spit and polish program to ready themselves, Reckless and the area for such a ceremony. A small reviewing stand was built, the citation, was written and the national and Marine Corps colors borrowed from regiment.

It was a colorful, impressive ceremony. With the company paraded, the General trooped the line and was then conducted to the platform. Lively and T/Sgt. Dave Woods escorted Reckless to proper position and Strange read the citation:

"For meritorious achievement in connection with operations against the enemy while serving with a Marine infantry regiment in Korea from October 26, 1952 to July 27, 1953. Corporal Reckless performed the duties of ammunition carrier in in a superb manner. Reckless' attention and devotion to duty make her well qualified for promotion to the rank of sergeant. Her absolute dependability while on missions under fire contributed materially to the success of many battles—"

General Pate pinned the stripes to the new blanket and Reckless became a sergeant in the Marine Corps. It was a happy day.

A short time later the General returned to Washington where he was promoted to lieutenant general and became assistant commandant. Reckless had a good friend in high places.

CHAPTER VII

EARLY IN DECEMBER the battalion commander returned from Kimpo to visit the Second and to say goodbye to Reckless. He had some pointed remarks to make to those concerned over the condition of her quarters and lack of attention to her feet. The situation was corrected with promptness.

Shortly after his return to the United States he had lunch with Ben Hibbs, editor of *The Saturday Evening Post*, and Reckless was discussed in detail. Hibbs asked that an article be prepared for *The Post*. This was done and the piece was scheduled for the April 17, 1954, issue.

At this time a letter was written to Colonel Victor "Brute" Krulak, staff secretary to the Commandant of the Marine Corps. The proposal was made to return Reckless to the States and to assign her to permanent duty at Camp Pendleton. The Brute was asked to intercede in her behalf at Headquarters.

With his usual energy and good nature, Krulak went to work on the problem. An answer came from Washington by return mail — and with it a chiding reminder that Reckless was not the first horse to serve with Marines in Korea:

"I was delighted to receive your letter and will take up the questions in order.

"First, as to the RECKLESS story in the Saturday Evening Post. I not only read it, but enjoyed it tremendously. It was warm and most convincing; beautifully done and sensitive.

"I regret to tell you that there is a terrible inaccuracy in the story. Reckless was by no means the first Marine horse of her type in Korea. In the spring of '51, when the Red Chinese withdrew northward for the last time, they left a great deal of material behind, as well as some transportation. Among other things which fell to the 1st Marine Division in its advance was a nice-looking light chestnut gelding, of about 15 hands and aged ten years. On his back was a very well-made English saddle, and he wore a good English bridle. He had two wounds in his near foreleg.

"He was seized upon by an enlisted man in the 1st Ordnance Battalion, who plastered the two wounds with athletes' foot ointment, and in a matter of a couple of weeks he was back on his feet. The boy gave the horse to me, and I rode him frequently in place of using a jeep in the rough, mountainous area where we were operating at that time.

"Unable to provide proper shoes for him, we made the best possible substitute out of composition soles from the Shoe and Textile Repair Unit. I have no doubt that he is the one and only horse ever to be so shod. The attached picture is furnished in the form of validation.

"There will be no charge for the secrecy which I intend to maintain regarding this fact.

"Be assured that I will commence investigation at once concerning the possibility of having Reckless returned. I have not the slightest idea what problems will be encountered, but will talk to Admiral Denebrink, who runs MSTS, which agency I feel would be the only possibility —"

There were stumbling blocks and time lags. Various departments at Headquarters Marine Corps were asked for opinions and possible public reaction to returning Reckless to the United States.

Colonel Raymond Crist of the Division of Public Information delivered the knockout punch in his evaluation of the project:

"In your letter you mentioned the problem of bringing Reckless to the United States. Marines who now have custody of Reckless are actually her legal owners, and they would have to be consulted before any action was taken to bring her to this country. Moreover, government transportation could only be furnished if this horse were owned by the Marine Corps. I realize that we possibly could buy the animal for one dollar, but I cannot see how we could justify the expense of transporting her to the United States for no other purpose than the attendant publicity. Even if we did overcome official objections and bring Reckless to this country, I am afraid that the publicity might be construed by some as Marine Corps assistance in the promotion of a commercial venture."

This was a disappointment. It was obvious by now that Reckless could not be furnished government transportation. A telephone call was put through to Ernest Gibson in the Operations Department of the Pacific Transport Lines. Gibson in turn discussed the matter with Stan Coppel, executive vice-president. Both of these men knew of Reckless through *The Saturday Evening Post* article. Within a few minutes the decision was made: Reckless could ride for free on any ship in the line. The only financial liability would be for her stall and feed. Gibson suggested the ship Pacific Transport due to sail from Yokohama on the twentieth of October be selected since Captain Kenneth Shannon, master of the vessel, loved horses and dogs. Shannon's pet Smokey, a black and white cocker, traveled aboard ship with his master and would be company for Reckless. Her hatred for dogs was not mentioned at this time.

An air mail, special delivery letter was sent off by Gibson to General Pate:

"I realized from the beginning that the Marine Corps would be open to censure if it expended public funds to return the little horse to the States. In my letter to "Brute" Krulak months ago I volunteered to pay the expenses.

"The legal ownership of Reckless rests with 1st Lt, Eric Pedersen, T/Sgt. Joseph Latham and PFC Monroe Coleman. It is unlikely any of the Marines now with Reckless were in the unit in October, 1952, when she was purchased. This is the account of the transaction: Pedersen bought her on the race track at Seoul on or about Oct. 26, 1952. With him at the time of the purchase were Sgt. Willard R. Berry and PFC Philip Carter. Berry was Pedersen's scout sergeant. It was Pedersen who had the pack saddle and other equipment purchased and flown to Korea at his own expense. That equipment is still with the unit. Pedersen paid $250. US for her.

"In April, 1953, when Pedersen was transferred he thought of taking the horse with him, but the men of the Recoilless Rifle Unit pleaded to let her remain with them. A collection was taken and Pedersen was partially repaid. Coleman and Latham still retain a monetary interest in Reckless. Pedersen's transfer took place nineteen months ago. In all likelihood there is no Marine in the AT unit who can claim he participated in the partial repayment.

"Additionally, I cannot see any Marine protesting her return if he is informed that she must remain behind when the Division departs Korea.

"Subject to your approval, I have made arrangements for Reckless to ride home on the freighter Pacific Transport. This ship sails from Yokohama on Oct. 22, and will arrive in San Francisco Nov. 5. Captain Shannon, master of the Pacific Transport, has assured me Reckless will be given the best care possible. At the Japanese end, the Marines handling the horse should contact Mr. G. K. Jones, Pacific Transport Lines, Tokyo. The phone number is 235153. He has already been notified to be on the lookout for her."

At the same time Gibson got off a letter to their representative in Yokohama, Gordon Jones:

"You will be approached by the Marine Corps, Tokyo, to make arrangements for transporting a famous horse from Yokohama to San

Francisco. The wheels are in motion to get Reckless aboard the SS Pacific Transport V/36E, due to sail yours 22, October, 1954.

"Contact in Tokyo will be through the First Marine Division Office (Finance Building):

'Colonel E. C. Ferguson, USMC
Representative Commanding General
Fleet Marine Force, Pacific
Far East Command
c/o Postmaster, San Francisco'

"The Marines will furnish a portable stall approximately 4 ft. wide by 10 ft. long with a sloping roof, f 6" high (front), 7' high (back), together with sufficient hay and oats for feeding and bedding down. If possible, a salt lick should also be provided. For protection from the weather it is suggested that the stall be placed as near aft of the house as possible.

"Stan Coppel has authorized deadhead transportation and the Marines have arranged here to pay the necessary charges for crew care (overtime for feeding and cleaning stall en route).

"In the event Reckless does not make the above sailing, please complete arrangements through Colonel Ferguson's office for any subsequent sailing, advising this office and the Master of whichever vessel is utilized."

By return mail Gibson received a letter from Jones:

"I refer to your letter, subject above, which was received on Sept. 21.

"I contacted Col. E. C. Ferguson who was both amused and surprised to learn about the pending shipment of Reckless to the States. I read the letter to him, to which he replied, and I quote: 'Do you realize, Mr. Jones, that I am here in the Finance Building in a small office with two Assistants and we haven't got a hammer, a saw or a nail in the place! How do they expect me to build a stall for a horse?'

"I had a copy of your letter made for the Colonel and I took it over to his office yesterday afternoon, but unfortunately the Colonel was out and I did not have the chance to meet him.

"The Colonel advised me on the telephone that he would look into the matter immediately and as soon as he receives some information, he would advise me.

"Rest assured that I shall keep in contact with Colonel Ferguson and that we shall cooperate with the Marine Corps to the fullest extent."

In the meantime, a letter was received from General Pate:

"I was most pleased to receive your letter of September 9, 1954, and to learn that you have been successful in working out plans to transport Reckless from Japan to San Francisco. I can see no cause for objection to your plan on the part of the Marine Corps.

"Am enclosing two pictures of the ceremony in which the little lady was made a sergeant."

With the receipt of General Pate's letter one was gotten off to Major General Robert E. Hogaboom, commanding the 1st Marine Division in Korea. Previous correspondence regarding Reckless was enclosed. Six days later a dispatch was received from Korea:

"1ST MARDIV AND 75 MM. R PLATOON 5TH MARINES WILLING TO SHIP RECKLESS ONLY UNDER THE FOLLOWING CONDITIONS X A X OWNERSHIP RESIDES WITH AND REMAINS IN 75 MM R PLATOON AT COMPANY 5TH MARINES THIS DIVISION X B X RECKLESS TO BE KEPT AT CAMP PENDLETON UNTIL SUCH TIME AS DIVISION RETURNS X C X ANY FUNDS ACCRUING HER NAME TO BE USED FOR DEPENDENTS OF DECEASED MEMBERS RR PLATOON AT COMPANY 5 TH MARINES X D X PFC MOORE MEMBER OF 75 MM RR PLATOON SINCE MARCH 53 AND PRESENT HANDLER OF RECKLESS SHOULD ACCOMPANY HER TO STATES IF YOU CAN ARRANGE X EARLY REPLY NECESSARY X MAJ-GEN HOGABOOM SENDS"

The matter of ownership was discussed with Pedersen by long distance telephone. He shared the feeling that the present members of the RR Platoon were being high-handed in the matter. As had been pointed out in earlier correspondence none of the present membership had been in Korea at the time Reckless was purchased. Contrary to the dispatch, PFC William Moore was not a member of the platoon until after the truce was signed.

Pedersen and the battalion commander agreed the matter could not be threshed out by telegram. The most important thing was to get Reckless aboard the Pacific Transport. All demands of the dispatch were agreed to and a ticket was purchased for Moore. Coppel apologized that he could not bring Moore home without charge, but he was prevented from this due to terms of a government mail subsidy contract.

In Korea, General Hogaboom queried the 1st Marine Aircraft Wing — could they provide air transportation for Reckless from Korea to Japan? This gave the logistics section of the Wing an unexpected and challenging training problem. This would be the first time they had been asked to airlift a horse in an R4Q (Flying Boxcar) aircraft. They had carried jeeps, 105 mm. howitzers, and every other conceivable load of war equipment, but never livestock. They fitted the problem into their training program.

The Chief of Staff of the Wing prepared a memorandum for the Chief of Staff of the Division:

"HEADQUARTERS

"1st Marine Aircraft Wing, FMF

"c/o Fleet Post Office, San Francisco

"16, October, 1954

"MEMORANDUM

"From: Chief of Staff, 1st Marine Aircraft Wing

"To: Chief of Staff, 1st Marine Division

"Subj: Operation HORSE SHIFT

"Ref: (a) CG, 1st Mar Div Memo of 12 Oct 54

"(b) CG, 1st MAW disp 130745Z Oct 54

"(c) Mar Corps GO No. 111

"1. Your request contained in reference (a) has been approved as indicated by reference (b). Certain personnel, logistical and medical details related to subject operation may have been overlooked by members of your staff and are cited for your action:

"a. Reference (a) failed to specify the sex of the passenger. It should be remembered that regulations require that female passengers in Naval aircraft must be suitably clothed in a trouser type uniform. Male passengers must be in the uniform of the day (ribbons optional). All passengers must wear dog tags and must be sober.

"b. In-flight box lunches are not furnished for passengers by this command. Present rations (Army common) do not include food fit for a horse. Recommend advice be obtained from the Army's First Cavalry Division.

"c. Although the responsibility for loading has been assumed by your headquarters, certain in-flight unloading problems must be anticipated. Responsibility for solution of these problems must naturally be assumed by you. A HORSE SHIFT Liaison Officer (hereafter referred to as DUNG-HO) is recommended.

"d. Close coordination between the pilot and DUNG-HO is required in this matter. Provisions must also be made for inspection by the Neutral Nations Inspection Team on return to Korea.

"e. Medical regulations require that passengers returning to CONUS must be dewormed and de-malariaized prior to departure. Compliance is requested in subject case.

"f. Passengers riding in the R4Q aircraft are required to don parachute harnesses prior to flight. This promises to be a difficult task, but the ingenuity of your staff is being counted on to find a solution.

"2. It is noted that paragraph 2 of reference (a) makes mention of precautions to insure safety of the animal in flight. While the sympathies of this command are solidly with Reckless, it must be remembered that the pilot will also be interested in maintaining the structural integrity of his aircraft. Therefore a horse adrift will be viewed with disfavor, and in case of unforeseen events he (or she) must be warned to stand clear of the pilots' compartment.

"(Signed)

"E. A. MONTGOMERY

"Chief of Staff."

The football season was in full play among the service teams in Korea and the game between the 7th Army Division and the 1st Marine Division was used as the appropriate time to announce the rotation of Reckless to the United States. With the drum and bugle corps to do the honors, she said good-by to the division.

"ROTATION CEREMONY

"(Half Time)

"1st Marine Division vs. 7th Army Division Football Game

"Oct. 17, 1954

"General Hogaboom, Officers and Men of the 1st Marine Division, guests and Sgt. Reckless, Pride of the Marines.

"Reckless began her career in the Marine Corps in October, 1952, when she was purchased in Seoul by the 75 mm. Recoilless Rifle Platoon of the Antitank Company, 5th Marines. Her boot camp was different from that of the ordinary Marine; she was trained to carry 75 Recoilless Rifle ammunition during actual combat. For outstanding conduct during this period, she was promoted to the rank of corporal.

"It was in the battle for the outpost Vegas that Reckless proved her merit as a Marine. With enemy artillery and mortar rounds coming in at the rate of 500 a minute, she carried 75 mm. shells into the front lines. Each yard as a passage under fire. Reckless made a total of fifty-one trips to the outpost during the Battle for Vegas to keep the guns supplied with ammunition.

"Disregard for her own safety and conduct under fire were an inspiration to the troops and in keeping with the highest traditions of the Naval Service.

"Corporal Reckless received her Meritorious Promotion to Sergeant on April 10, 1954. The citation reads in part, 'Cpl. Reckless performed the duties of ammunition carrier from October, 1952, to July 27, 1953, in a superb manner. Reckless' attention and devotion to duty make her well qualified for promotion to the rank of sergeant. Her absolute dependability while on missions under fire contributed materially to the success of many battles.'

"Rotation to the United States is her due and in a few weeks she will be on her way to Camp Pendleton — home of the 1st Marine Division. Good luck, Sergeant Reckless, and Bon Voyage."

As soon as it was known that Reckless was to meet the ship, word was passed to General Pate as well as Pedersen, Lively, Coleman, Latham and Mull. Pedersen and Lively responded that they would be in San Francisco to meet her with a trailer to carry her back to Camp Pendleton. Coleman, now out of the Corps, wrote he would drive to the coast from Utah. Latham and Mull telephoned Pedersen they would make every effort to cross the country from Camp Lejeune, North Carolina.

Major General Evans Ames, managing director of the Marines Memorial Club, issued an invitation for Reckless to attend the Marine Corps Birthday banquet to be held the night of the tenth of November. The invitation was accepted by proxy.

A telephone call was put through to the U. S. Customs Service.

"What duty, if any, would have to be paid on a Marine war horse?"

"What horse?"

"A Korean horse named Reckless."

"That the horse I read about in *The Saturday Evening Post?*"

"The same."

"Very easy, Colonel Bring a set of your orders down and bring her in as part of your baggage. Either that or declare her being worth fifty dollars and we'll charge you $3.75."

"Okay, I'll do it that way, but don't let Reckless or any of her Marine friends know I put that valuation on her."

The United States Agriculture Department was difficult. Their procedure was involved. The animal's feet would have to be inspected on board ship by a bureau veterinarian; a sample of blood would have to be drawn and sent to Washington, D. C, for analysis. Tests would be run for dourine and glanders. (All hands were highly indignant when the meaning of dourine was discovered.)

The "animal" would have to remain aboard or on the dock until clearance was received.

"Isn't there a laboratory in California certified to make such an analysis?"

"No!"

"Why?"

"That's the way it has been done for fifty years."

"In other words, Reckless might have to live aboard ship or on the dock for a week after she gets into port?"

"If you'll pay air-mail charges, it will only take about seventy-two hours."

"Yes, but she's been invited to a banquet on the evening of the 10th. She has to get out of quarantine right away."

"She has to what?"

"Go to a banquet. She's to be the honored guest."

"You'll be liable to a heavy fine if you try to take her off without permission."

"Who is your head man in Washington?"

"Dr. C. L. Gooding, Chief Animal Inspection Quarantine Branch, Agriculture Research Service."

A telegram was sent off to Dr. Gooding:

"IMPORTING HORSE JAPAN SAN FRANCISCO. ANIMAL CARE FIRST MARINE DIVISION SINCE OCTOBER 52. TO FACILITATE REMOVAL PORT OF ENTRY TO PERMANENT QUARTERS, CAMP PENDLETON, OCEANSIDE, CALIFORNIA, WOULD YOU ACCEPT CERTIFIED BLOOD SAMPLE AIRMAILED FROM YOKOHAMA. CERTIFICATION BY SENIOR MARINE OFFICER JAPAN AREA."

Some headway was made in Washington, however, by permission for her to leave the dock. At least, she was assured of being able to go to the banquet.

"BRANCH NOT IN POSITION TO ACCEPT BLOOD SAMPLE FROM JAPAN. WILL PERMIT HORSE TO PROCEED CAMP PENDLETON FOLLOWING COLLECTION OF SAMPLE AT SAN FRANCISCO IF OTHERWISE ELIGIBLE FOR ENTRY WITH UNDERSTANDING IF POSITIVE REACTION DOURINE OR

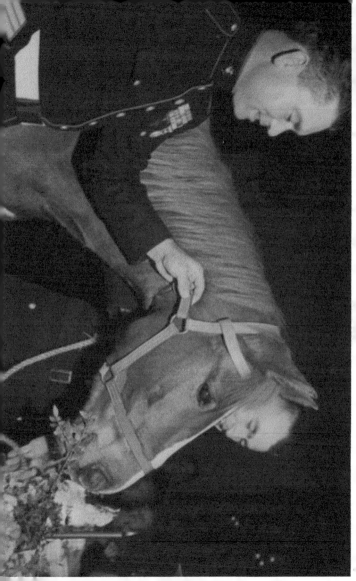

GLANDERS ANIMAL WILL BE DESTROYED OR IMMEDIATELY RETURNED TO JAPAN."

Not many days later Captain Shannon reported the ship in a typhoon. The Marines who knew Reckless and remembered her trip with the Navy wondered if she were sick again. She was.

Meantime, various news media were informed that Reckless was en route. Bob Considine, noted newspaperman, launched her welcome home campaign over his coast-to-coast radio broadcast. This was followed by a column on her.

Ed Sullivan of the *New York Daily News* and *Toast of the Town* TV program, also wrote a column and sent a telegram:

"I HAVE WRITTEN MY SUNDAY NOVEMBER SEVENTH COLUMN ABOUT RECKLESS AS PART OF MY ANNUAL OBSERVANCE OF THE MARINE CORPS ANNIVERSARY. I'D LIKE VERY MUCH TO HAVE RECKLESS APPEAR ON OUR STAGE NOVEMBER SEVENTH AS GENERAL DEVEREAUX WILL BE IN OUR AUDIENCE THAT NIGHT. HOW MUCH WOULD IT COST TO SEND HER EAST? IN ADDITION TO TRANSPORTATION I WILL EARMARK AN EXTRA ONE THOUSAND DOLLARS FOR YOUR FUND FOR MARINE FAMILIES. WIRE ME.

"SINCERELY ED SULLIVAN."

The ship was delayed by the storm and Sullivan was notified Reckless could not make the show.

Governor Goodwin J. Knight took time out from his campaign for re-election to issue a proclamation welcoming her to California:

"Executive Department

"State of California

"November 2, 1954

"Californians are proud to join with our United States Marines in welcoming Sergeant Reckless home from Korea.

"Fighting with our men of the First Division this great-hearted little mare became the symbol of their spirit. During the bitter days, while carrying ammunition to the Reckless Rifles of the First, she was twice wounded. Yet, despite her bloodied flanks, she continued to plod the Korean hills. Such courage understandably won the respect of the men who know courage best.

"Therefore, I am proud California has been chosen as home for this heroic animal.

"I know the years ahead will hold affection for her by those who fought beside her. But more important, as time goes on, this little mare with the blaze will mingle with Marines-yet-to-be and, in her inimitable way, instill in them the spirit of Semper Fidelis; life's breath to the Eternal Corps.

"Goodwin J. Knight

"Governor of California

"(SEAL)"

Pedersen and Lively arrived from Camp Pendleton with the trailer. Coleman and bride arrived from Utah. Latham and Mull wired it was impossible for them to make it. The night before the ship arrived the Marines had a meeting to plan the reception for their friend. In the midst of this gathering the telephone rang. It was Captain Shannon on the radio telephone. A nervous hush settled on the group. What had happened? It must be Reckless!

Shannon's voice came over weakly, "Colonel, I thought I should call you about Reckless."

"What is it? What happened?"

"In case you're planning a parade or anything ..." Shannon's voice faded.

"Yes, Captain, what is it? What did you say?"

Slowly the bad news was transmitted and the connection broken. The older officer returned to the room with the other Marines. Their eyes were on him.

"Bad news?" Pedersen asked.

"Yes! Reckless ate her blanket, even the ribbons. All that's left are a few rags."

"I told them that would happen the first day she wore the blanket! That Moore must be a first-class idiot to leave it where she could get hold of it." Lively's mood indicated he would have words with Moore.

"The other night in the storm she got swept out of her stall and they found her sprawled on deck ready to go over the side."

Pedersen's reaction to the near accident summed up the feelings of all, "Going over the side wouldn't phase her any. She'd probably beat the ship into port."

"With every photographer in town on the dock, we've got to get a blanket for her, and we've got to work fast. Eric, when you go to the airport to meet Kay in the morning you'll see a saddlery shop on Third Street. It's an old San Francisco landmark — Olsen Nolte is the name.

They should have what we want. While you're doing that Jane will find a lettering outfit to sew on what we want. I'll get the ribbons made up. Other than that, we're in good shape. A Lieutenant Newell, veterinarian from the Presidio, has volunteered to meet her and draw the blood."

"When does the ship arrive?"

"The captain said about 5:30 or 6:00 in the afternoon. After Newell has drawn the blood and the Agriculture people have looked at her feet, we'll take her to Golden Gate Park for exercise."

All plans had to be canceled. Inspector Eddy of the Agriculture Department informed Gibson that the ship was docking after the normal closing time of 5:00 o'clock. If the animal were to be inspected, overtime and travel pay would have to be paid to himself and a bureau veterinarian. Such service would cost $30 to $40. The decision was made that Reckless would remain aboard ship for the night.

The day of arrival was a busy one. Pedersen and Lively called on Olsen Nolte. Creed Haberlin, the manager, had read of her arrival. He donated a blanket, halter, curry comb and brush and foot pick.

Haberlin told Pedersen, "My kids have been reading about her. If I didn't do something for her they wouldn't let me in the house."

It is said by some who know horses that they have little intelligence and no memory but these detractors had never met Reckless. When the Marines appeared on the hatch they found her straining over the crossbar of the stall. She nodded to Lively, Coleman and Pedersen in turn. It was apparent to anyone who witnessed the meeting that she knew them and was delighted to see them again. It was a scene to be remembered and all were sorry Latham could not have been there.

Shortly after daylight the Marines were back aboard preparing her for the photographers. Her feet were cleaned and the hoofs polished and the three white stockings and blaze washed with shampoo. Newell arrived early with bottles and needles, but the blood sample could not be drawn until the government officials arrived.

In no time she could have passed a general's inspection and was ready to meet the press. Eddy and his bureaucratic mate from the Agriculture Department arrived and stood by while Newell drew the blood. The young officer was concerned lest Reckless should rear and strike her head on the deck housing overhang when he inserted the needle.

Pedersen told him, "Go ahead, she won't even nod." Newell shrugged and placed his barracks cap on a fender and gave the neck several sharp pats to numb it.

Reckless paid him no heed whatsoever. She had just finished a carrot when she saw the barracks cap. While Newell rammed the needle home and the blood began to flow into the bottle, she reached over his shoulder and grabbed the cap. Lively rescued it in time to save it from going the way of so many things. Eddy took the sample and departed.

Reckless was then free of red tape and ready to meet the press. By this time the ship was crowded with photographers and reporters.

As one veteran newsman observed, "She has more cameras and reporters to meet her than Vice-President Nixon had a week ago when he came to town."

Reckless appeared to enjoy it. She posed with various Marines, she ate carrots, she walked into and out of her stall a dozen times while flash bulbs popped and cameramen shouted for different poses. Then she became bored and let Pedersen know it. She was placed in an unloading stall and with Pedersen at her head, the winch swung her over the side and lowered her to the dock. Fourteen months after she had been promised a home in California she arrived.

The newsreel and TV cameramen were entranced with such a beautifully poised subject. Later in the day they met with her on the stage of the Marines' Memorial Club where she was toasted and, in turn, toasted many new friends — all with cola. She also drank a glass of milk in case the soft drink should look like an alcoholic beverage in the pictures.

There were some who doubted her behavior in the elevator which she would have to ride to gain the tenth-floor banquet hall. She confounded her skeptics in San Francisco as she had in Korea. She rode the elevator as though she owned it. She walked into a banquet hall where four hundred people waited for her and flashbulbs popped like mortar shells along the MLR. She stood at the head table and ate cake. When there was no more cake she started in on the rose and carnation table decorations.

Still later she appeared in the ballroom for the official cake cutting ceremony. As is traditional in the Marine Corps, the first slice was given to the most honored Marine present. In this instance there was no one to dispute her right. It was fitting she should eat it from the hand of Kay Pedersen. She was the belle of the ball and it was after midnight before Lively and Pedersen escorted her to her quarters on Pier Seven.

The next day was equally busy. In the morning she was taken to the San Francisco Cow Palace to have a run. She put on one of her greatest performances — the rocking horse strut, the whirling run, the charge at Pedersen as though to run him down, the stiff-legged bucking action.

That afternoon she went to the exclusive Bohemian Club to meet the membership. It was a Thursday and the Cartoon Room was crowded when she made her entrance. It was the first time in the long history of the club that a lady had been admitted to the clubrooms. After a pleasant time, she and Lively and Pedersen said goodbye to the battalion commander and departed for Camp Pendleton.

A letter was prepared to the Commandant of the Marine Corps relative to the future of Reckless.

"November 19, 1954

"From: Lt Col. Andrew C. Geer 025898/0302 USMCR

"To: Commandant of the Marine Corps

"Headquarters, U. S. Marine Corps

"Washington 25, D. C.

"Subj: SERGEANT RECKLESS

"Ref: (a) CG, 1st Mar. Div. Dis 050706Z

"1. Reference (a) established the willingness of the Commanding General of the First Marine Division and members of the 75 mm. Recoilless Rifle Platoon of the Fifth Marines to ship Reckless to the United States providing certain guarantees were made by the undersigned. These were: (a) The ownership of Reckless would reside with the 75mm. Recoilless Rifle Platoon Antitank Company Fifth Marines, (b) That Reckless be stationed at Camp Pendleton until such time as the First Marine Division returns from Korea, (c) That any funds accruing to her through public appearances be used for dependents of deceased members of the Recoilless Rifle Platoon, (d) That PFC William Moore accompany her to the United States.

"2. The undersigned, readily agreed to the ownership clause inasmuch as his sole interest was to see the horse safely in the United States. However, it is felt the claim of ownership by the present membership of the Platoon is tenuous and unfair. No member of this unit was in Korea at the time Reckless joined, and none participated in the partial repayment of Lieutenant Eric Pedersen's original outlay. PFC Moore's claim to have been in the RR Platoon since March, 1953, is fatuous. He joined the RR Platoon after the truce was signed. Let us say her ownership rests with the hundreds of Marines, living and dead, who were at the Battle of Vegas, where she won their love by her valiant service.

"3. STATION, CARE AND FEEDING OF SGT. RECKLESS

"a. The undersigned is in hearty agreement that Reckless should be stationed at Camp Pendleton, as indicated in Paragraph (b) of reference (a). It should be kept in mind, however, that this is no ordinary horse and she should have special care and attention. She should have a large and luxurious box stall constructed for living quarters. Her pasture should be commodious and watered to provide the best grass. It is suggested her "court" be in the vicinity of the Commanding General's quarters and properly marked with appropriate sign, so that all will know this to be the home of Sergeant Reckless, Pride of the Marines. As long as Lieutenant Pedersen and Sergeant Elmer Lively are stationed at Camp Pendleton, they should be assigned the additional duty of caring for their friend. Never should she be ridden by oversized, leaden-seated, heavy-handed cowboy types, nor should she ever be considered one of the post stable horses.

"b. Due to an injury suffered in Korea when hit by a jeep, she has a weakened left hip and overwork will bring on lameness. She should never be ridden by anyone weighing in excess of 130 pounds and then only enough for exercise and light training. Every six months she should have a thorough physical examination. She likes children and is gentle in their presence. Because of her having been savaged by wild Korean dogs, she is committed to the destruction of the canine race and dogs should be kept clear.

"c. Upon being turned to pasture in Pendleton, her shoes should be removed and she should be allowed to go barefoot for a period of six weeks. At that time her feet should be trimmed and new shoes fitted. Only the most knowing and patient horseshoer should be employed. Sergeant Reckless is extremely proud of her feet and will not stand for inexpert attention. Several Korean horseshoers will painfully attest to this statement. She should be groomed each day and her mane and tail, which have become ragged by inexpert clipping and, perhaps, a dietary deficiency, should be encouraged by daily brushing. The Headquarters Duty Officer should be directed to inspect her and her quarters once in each twenty-four-hour period.

"d. Flame of the Morning knew hardship, but never cruelty before joining the Corps. Her Korean owner was a skilled horseman with the hands that come to one man in ten thousand. But for the sad state to which the Korean war had brought him, Lieutenant Pedersen would never have been able to buy her that October day in 1952. Reckless learned to trust man through this kindly Korean. Because of this trust she will go anywhere and do anything man suggests, if she likes the man. That is why she would crawl into a jeep trailer and ride some thirty rough miles the first time she saw Pedersen; why she would make repeated trips into the MLR under the heaviest bombardments of incoming with PFC Coleman; why she would crowd into a small elevator and ride upwards eleven floors and walk nonchalantly into a banquet hall packed with people the first day she was in the United States.

"e. This does not mean she likes all Marines just because they are Marines. During the days of fighting in Korea she had her favorites in the RR platoon and among members of the 2nd Battalion 5th Marines. There were also members of both units over whom she would not pine if they were transferred. Therefore, the selection of the Marine to see after her must be made with care. Being of a positive disposition, she will let all hands know if she does not cotton to a certain individual.

"During the extreme heat of Korea, when potable water was scarce or nonexistent, Reckless came to know and like certain liquids other than water. She is fond of coca cola and milk, even the powdered variety. Under the stress of battle she has been known to drink beer. However, all liquids should be served in a common variety water glass. When drinking from a bottle she has been known to bite off the top and this could prove injurious. Cola in limited amounts (no more than two or three glasses a week) could be provided. Of milk she should have all she and the budget will stand. As a change from her usual ration of grain and alfalfa she can be served an occasional plate of scrambled eggs lightly salted and without pepper. She also relishes carrots, apples, sugar and kimchi, although it is unlikely this latter food will be found in southern California.

"g. Reckless will not take salt from a lick. It must be placed in her grain or on her eggs and never too much at one time.

"4. Paragraph (c) of reference (a) pertaining to the disposition of funds earned by Sergeant Reckless through television, moving picture appearances, etc., was agreed to by the undersigned because it would have taken too much time to discuss the matter by dispatches between Korea and California. The request by the RR Platoon to have all monies earned allocated to dependents of deceased members of the platoon is unrealistic. An organization would have to be formed with a bonded treasurer appointed to handle and dispense funds so earned. It is pointed out that from the time Reckless joined the RR Platoon on the 26th of October, 1952, until the Korean Truce was signed in July of 1954, no member of the Platoon suffered a fatality. Obviously, no one is eligible.

"a. It is recommended that such funds as may be earned by Sergeant Reckless be placed in the Korean Fund of the First Marine Division Association which is set up for the assistance and education of dependents of Marines killed in Korea. This recognized charitable organization is already in existence and functioning.

"5. PERSONAL APPEARANCES OF SGT. RECKLESS AND CONTROL THEREOF

"a. A committee of four to handle her public appearances should be formed. It is recommended that this group include: (1) Director of Public Information, Headquarters, U. S. Marine Corps; (2) Marine Corps Public Information Officers in New York and Los Angeles and the Commanding General at Camp Pendleton. The undersigned offers his services as special advisor.

"b. In connection with the public appearance of Reckless, she should never be subjected to appearing on a program which will not lend dignity to this gallant warrior. She should not be asked to appear on commercially sponsored programs of the beer, wine or liquor industry. She will endorse certain products (horse feed, milk, cola) only after thorough research establishes she really likes the product and the concern involved is of good reputation. Reckless should be available without charge to worthy charities, such as Navy Relief, March of Dimes and American-Korean Foundation.

"c. Care should be exercised in television and moving picture commitments. As a case in point: One Hollywood producer was ecstatic over the idea of having Reckless do a talking mule type of routine, a la Francis. Such antics may be all right for the Army, but there is as much difference between Sgt. Reckless and Francis as there is between a horse and a mule. After all, one is a Hollywood clown and the other a gallant Marine who won honors in one of the bloodiest battles fought by American troops.

"d. Also, a television producer wished to star Sgt. Reckless in a twenty-six-episode program, the film to be sold at considerable profit to himself and his company. When asked how much he would donate to the Marine Fund, his reply was, "Nothing." He was informed that this was the exact amount of footage he would be allowed to shoot. Obviously, if Reckless is to appear without pay on one commercial program, a donation cannot be asked of another. Therefore, television appearances should be carefully screened. At the moment, she is a sought-after celebrity. It is recommended that the fee for a personal appearance or endorsement of a product be set at $1,000. This will weed out all but those with a sincere desire to show her to the American people.

"e. The forthcoming book *Sergeant Reckless*, dealing with her life, will add further luster to her name. It should also bring moving picture and television offers. With her beauty, poise and intelligence, the undersigned sees no reason why she should not portray herself. Given a reasonable explanation of what is expected, she will do most anything. After all, she crawled into a jeep trailer at first asking. Life in Hollywood, over an extended period, is not recommended, but it is possible she would find a few weeks interesting and profitable.

"6. FUTURE LIFE AND POSSIBLE MATING

"a. Careful thought should be given to mating Reckless with a suitable stallion. Its qualifications must be of the highest and only the finest should be considered. Reckless' mate should not be a large animal. It is recommended the Morgan or Arabian strain be searched for a worthy suitor. Because of my love for this little horse, it is requested that the first colt be mine, for which I will pay all stud fees and attendant expenses and donate to the Fund whatever sum is decided upon by the Commandant of the Marine Corps.

"b. With good fortune and loving care Reckless should live many years and produce several foals, so that her legend will not die. No better sentiment has been expressed than in Governor Goodwin J. Knight's proclamation welcoming her to the State of California. The Governor closed with these words:

'I know the years ahead will hold affection for her by those who fought beside her. But more important, as time goes by, this little mare with the blaze will mingle with Marines-yet-to-be and, in her inimitable way, instill in them the spirit of Semper Fidelis, life's breath to the Eternal Corps.'

"Andrew C. Geer

"2320 Leavenworth Street

"

San Francisco, California"

A short time later an answer was received from Reckless' old friend. There was no doubt her treatment would be that of a VIP.

"DEPARTMENT OF THE NAVY

"Headquarters United States Marine Corps

"Washington 25, D. C.

"My dear Colonel:

Your letter of November 19, 1954, addressed to the Commandant, has been read with considerable interest, and your thoughts concerning the care and welfare of Sergeant Reckless are heart-warming, especially to the many veterans of the 1st Marine Division who share your admiration for this courageous Korean veteran.

"A copy of your letter is being forwarded to General Hogaboom requesting his comments on those portions dealing with the contractual agreements concerning her. It is hoped that mutually satisfactory terms may be worked out. A copy is also going to the Commanding General at the Marine Corps Base, Camp Pendleton, requesting his comment and recommendations with regard to the special handling and care you have suggested. Please feel at liberty to visit Major General Selden to discuss personally with him any questions which he may have incident to your recommendations.

"Your offer to become a special advisor to any committee formed to handle her public appearances is sincerely appreciated. Although your suggested committee parallels the normal chain of command and, therefore, would not appear to be entirely necessary, we will request your generously offered advice whenever public appearances are contemplated.

"I am confident that arrangements can be completed at Camp Pendleton which will ensure that Sergeant Reckless may enjoy the care and the surroundings which her faithful service in Korea justifies.

"Sincerely yours,

"R. McC. Pate

"Lieutenant General, U. S. Marine Corps

"Assistant Commandant of the Marine Corps"

Major General John Taylor Selden, commanding general of Camp Pendleton, said of her reception.

"I was at the main entrance to meet Sergeant Reckless. She is every bit as beautiful and well trained as I had been told. Although she joined the Division after I had turned over command to Al Pollock, I have heard from many Marines about her valiant service in Korea. It was with pride I welcomed her to Camp Pendleton.

"After she met the guard, we drove to the Ranch House where she met Mrs. Selden. It was a case of love at first sight for both. We had Reckless make her mark in the guest book and if it hadn't been for Lt. Pedersen, she would have eaten the pen.

"As for her future, I can assure that there are twenty-five thousand Marines on this base who are determined she will want for nothing — ever. When the 1st Marine Division returns from Korea that number will be doubled. Need I say more?"

Made in the USA
Columbia, SC
10 December 2019